prayers *for* everyday living

Jewel g.

JEWELLYN GREER

prayers
for
everyday
living

Words of Encouragement
to Refresh and Comfort You

TATE PUBLISHING & *Enterprises*

Published by Tate Publishing & Enterprises, LLC
127 E. Trade Center Terrace | Mustang, Oklahoma 73064 USA
1.888.361.9473 | www.tatepublishing.com

Tate Publishing is committed to excellence in the publishing industry. The company reflects the philosophy established by the founders, based on Psalm 68:11,
"The Lord gave the word and great was the company of those who published it."

Book design copyright © 2011 by Tate Publishing, LLC. All rights reserved.
Cover design by Amber Gulilat
Interior design by Nathan Harmony

Published in the United States of America

ISBN: 978-1-61777-879-7
1. Religion / General
2. Religion / Christian Life / Prayer
11.06.16

Acknowledgments

This book is dedicated to the memory of my Grandmother Tatmon. She loved the Lord, loved to sing but did not know how to read, was blind and hard of hearing, and she referred to me as her eyes and her ears. I would take her to church, read the Bible to her, and sing for her. I was lucky enough to grow up in an extended family environment, and even though my mother was at home, my grandmother took on a motherly role in my upbringing. Oh, I gave her a lot of trouble growing up, mainly because she spoiled me, and I just wish that she was alive today to see the woman that I have become, to see that all that she was trying to teach me, and the instructions she gave me from an early age are being manifested now. I know that she is always silently watching over me.

I also want to acknowledge my mother, Sarah Greer, affectionately known as Mommy Toodie. She has been a mother and father to all seven of us, and she has done a remarkable job. Mommy, I speak for all of us. You should pat yourself on your back because you did a wonderful job. You gave us the necessary tools to prepare us for the lives we are living today. I remember how you encouraged us through praying at home, reading the Bible, attending church, Sunday school, and giving us the best of everything. Looking back, I did not know where this encouragement was leading to, because I always loved to sing and to read, and you encouraged that 100 percent. I would sing while washing dishes and you would join in. You had a regular book salesman who came to our home, we had reading time and we were regular readers in church. I will remember this one day for the rest of my life, which I believed in part was responsible for my successful career as a journalist: One Sunday, it was my turn to read the lesson at church and I got scared and could not continue and started to cry. My mother, I recall was so upset, that I was disciplined right there in church, not because she was embarrassed, but because, in her words, "I know how well she could read, and I know that she is not a shy person outside of church." From that day till now, I don't think that there is any audience that could intimidate me. Thanks, Mommy. I love you.

I want to especially thank my daughter, Davika, and my family and friends for supporting and encouraging me. I am continually thanking God for you, for your prayers, for your financial, emotional, and physical support throughout the years.

There are those who I would like to thank for giving me a push in life that I could never repay, and you know who you are; you are too numerous to single out. For my mentors who believed in me when I did not believe in myself when I started out as a radio announcer, for those who took a chance on me, a foreigner in a strange land, for those who were not quick to judge me because of my faults, you know that my praise is heartfelt. This book is a tribute to all of you, and my humble way of thanking you.

I also want to acknowledge Pastor Charles Stanley of In Touch Ministries. Pastor Stanley, if I get to heaven and you are not there, you had better be right behind me, because you have been inspiring me throughout my walk with God. I admire you as a preacher who is like no other I have ever encountered. Thank you for the opportunity to listen to you each week on the television, and for your Bible studies that have helped me to grow in my walk with God. I am striving daily to build a life message through my character, conduct, and conversations. Thank you.

Finally, I want to give thanks and high praise to God, who has given me this inspiration for this book, who has opened this door of opportunity for me, who has set limits for me that man can't reach. You may wonder why He is last on my acknowledgments page. I will tell you, because this is just the beginning. I am on a spiritual journey with my God, who I know is the Author and Finisher of everything. He is first in my heart; He knows that I am full of praise to Him for the wonderful things He is doing in my life. He is just smiling down at me, because from the moment He placed this dream in my heart, I never doubted that it would become a reality. Oh, thank You, Jesus, that I am living by faith and not by sight, that I know eyes have not seen nor ear heard, nor has it entered into the heart of man, what You have in store for me. I am trusting You with my whole heart.

Contents

A Word of Encouragement for My Readers

Prayer and faith in God changes everything. I know because I have been prayerful and faithful to God, and He has rewarded me bountifully. When you pray, you must believe and never doubt; your faith should never waver. You should be prayerful in good times and in bad times; you must be faithful to God always. When I pray and doubt, I get confused and disappointed, but when I pray and believe and wait patiently on the Lord, my prayers are answered. We must learn to pray about everything, putting God front and center of all of our needs, all of our decisions, all of our choices, allowing God to intercede on our behalf, and He will always lead us into greener pastures. He will not cause our feet to slide. He will not withhold anything good from us. We will always have enough. Your friends will want to know the secret of your success and the source of your joy. You just tell them to taste and see that the Lord is good. Tell them about your awesome God and what He has done for you. Tell them that you serve a God of second chances, a God who is full of kindness and always ready to forgive, a God of provisions, healing and deliverance, He is your all in all. Tell them to pray without ceasing, and with faith believing, learning to listen to the voice of God, and to wait patiently for Him to act.

Introduction

This is my testimony that I want to share with you my readers. I completed a Bible study early in my Christian life, and to conclude the study, I had to ask myself and answer some challenging questions, which has given me a better understanding of myself and where I am in my walk with God, and that being said "I will share with you what God has done for me, and maybe one day you will share with me what God has done for you."

Are you a Christian? Yes, I am a Christian.

How do you know that you are a Christian? I know that I am a Christian, because not only do I have a testimony, but I am able to proudly share the good news of Christ.

How do you become a Christian? To be a Christian means that you must first accept the Lord as your personal Savior. You must be willing to walk in His ways and to do His will.

How long has it been since you accepted the Lord as your personal Savior? Eight years.

How do you view life as a Christian? It is awesome. Living the Christian life is both challenging and rewarding. Being a Christian means that you must always be obedient to God, and being obedient to God requires much *faith*, and without *faith*, it is absolutely impossible to please God.

Have you always been obedient to God? No, but I will say this, "The steps of a good man are ordered by the Lord, and if you trust Him, though you may stumble, you will not utterly be cast down, for the Lord will hold you up"

(Psalm 37:23–24). I view my life as a broken vessel that is sent to the potter's house repeatedly for repairs. As children of God we make choices daily, and I think that the most important choices we should make as Christians, is to choose between the right and the wrong. It is not always easy, as many times instead of listening to God and turning to Him for directions, we follow the devises of our own hearts, which has dire consequences. I am only human, and I will admit that when I stumble, I am honest enough to come boldly before the presence of God and ask for His forgiveness and His guidance.

Are you setting an example for others by being a Christian? I strive to set an example for others by serving God, through my character, conduct, and conversations. My character determines who I am; my conduct determines what I do, and my conversations represent what I say. My goal is to strive every day to build a life message that will be pleasing to God, through my character, conduct, and conversations.

Are you promoting a ministry for God? God gives us all talents that He wants us to use for His glory. I have been blessed with vocal talents. I can sing, I can read, and I can pray. I can also write. I currently serve on the prayer and healing team at my church, where I also sing solos during the eight o'clock mass. I have not been using my gift of reading as much for the glory of God, and I intend to change that. In the past I have been a journalist, celebrity reader in schools, and I loved reading and singing to my grandmother when she was alive. I write prayers, songs, and poems but have not had the opportunity to share with others until now. I have always had a gift to bring comfort to others, and over the years, this has grown into a ministry of its own: *A Ministry of Being There.*

Do you have a testimony that you would like to share? I have testimonies that I could share with you that would take all day, but what I would like to share today is my testimony of faith:

My friends, it is *impossible* to serve and to please God without *faith*. During my walk with God, I have learned the importance of trusting God for everything. As you go through your struggles each day, no matter what you need, no matter how dismal the situation, keep reminding yourself and believe in your heart, that your God will supply all that you need according to His riches in glory in Christ Jesus. Remind yourself that you are a child of God, and that He has promised to never leave you nor forsake you; therefore, you must "be strong in the Lord and in the strength of His might" (Ephesians 6:10). Know that God is able to accomplish infinitely more than you could ever dare to ask or hope for.

That being said, I will tell you of what God has been able to accomplish in my life, since I invited Him into my heart, and trusted Him completely. The Lord *humbled me.* Words cannot describe what change that action has brought to my life. I could not understand it then, but I know now, that the first thing that needed to be changed in my life, was to be *humble.*

Since then, my God pulled me out of the miry clay; my God has made a path for me where there was no path; my God has opened doors for me that man can't shut; my God has delivered me from storms that should have destroyed me; my God has prepared a table before me in the presence of my enemies; my God is daily removing fear and doubt from within me; my God is making every crooked path in my life straight. I have a constant hungering and thirsting for God. I praise Him in good times and in bad times. I bring all my burdens to Him. I make all my petitions to Him and trust Him for the right answer at the right time. There is a song in my heart always. He satisfies my life with good things; He is leading me in green pastures.

My friends, learn to delight yourself in the Lord, and He will give you the desires of your heart. The road ahead will not be easy, but always remember, that no matter how long or dark the road may be, you are not alone, and that God will give you strength and courage for the journey. So give Him your heart, and ask Him to create in you a clean heart, and to renew a right Spirit within You. Amen.

Praise and Worship

On Fire for God

We have too often been described as lukewarm Christians. This prayer explains how on fire for God I am as a Christian—you could be too.

Dear God, I am so thankful that I could express my emotions for You without fear or shame. I am so thankful that I feel on fire for You always. I now understand what it means to be on fire for You, and what I need to do to stay on fire for You. I express my feelings for You in so many different ways each day.

When I am on fire for You oh God, I express the feeling of always wanting to share the good news of Christ. I have a constant hunger and thirst for You. There is always a song of praise in my heart and I have an intimate relationship with You where I can commune with You day and night, in good times and in bad times.

I stay on fire for You oh God, by expressing my love for You in so many ways: by loving others, by promoting ministries for You oh God, by always feasting and meditating on Your Word, and by asking for Your guidance in my daily walk with You.

I stay on fire for You oh God by being a friend of the friendless, by praying for and helping someone in need, by learning, not to only bring my petitions to You oh God, but knowing just how to give You thanks and praise for

Your goodness and mercy toward me, and learning to be still in Your presence.

I understand now oh God, that to be on fire for You requires a strong belief, a clean heart, and a pure conscience; that when I am on fire for You, I could be in the midst of a storm and singing Your praises. When I am on fire for You oh God, my way is dark, but You guide me in Your marvelous light.

When I am on fire for You oh God, others are happy to be in my presence. When I am on fire for You oh God, others see Christ in me. When I am on fire for You oh God, I could help to lead others to Christ, by living a life that is holy and blameless and acceptable before You.

I am so glad that I am on fire for God.

Give God a Praise

So many times we have prayed to God to help us, and we forget to lift Him up in praise when He answers our prayers. I am guilty, because there have been times when I have forgotten to thank God for answering my prayers—this could easily happen if your prayer need at the time is not significant. We must remember to thank God for small mercies.

Stop right where you are and give God a praise, don't think; just stop right where you are and give God a praise. You have been blessed. You have been blessed in so many ways. But did you stop? Did you stop to give God a praise?

There were times when you were down, when you were standing on shaky ground, when your back was against the wall, when you were just about to fall, something or someone picked you up, and set you straight again.

That *something* was Jesus. That *someone* was Jesus. If you did not know it then, you know it now. So stop right where you are, and give God a praise.

You were sick, you were in need, you prayed for God to intercede, you were highly favored, you were healed, your strength was renewed, but did you stop to give God a praise?

Did you stop; did you stop to give God a praise? Stand right where you are, stand right where you are, and give God a praise.

Pause for a moment and think of something that you could praise God for today.

Nothing but Praise
for God

You are in a good place if you could just have a praise for God and no complaints. I recall many times in my walk with God when I was always in need, always complaining, but there are some days that I have nothing but praise for God. It's an awesome feeling.

Where do I begin to praise God today? I feel so good just to be in His presence. I have a smile on my face and a song in my heart. Today, I am feeling spiritually wealthy. I have nothing but praise for God.

Lord, look where you brought me from. A few months ago, I was singing, but not as sweetly. I now feel free in spirit, mind, and body. I sit here trying to find something wrong in my life to pray for, and I have nothing but praise on my lips.

I am so thankful when I remember all that the Lord has done for me; when I see where He brought me from; I was so broke, busted, and confused. My bills were overwhelming; problems assailed me from every side; but I trusted in You, oh Lord, I trusted You with my whole heart. I waited patiently on You all the daylong.

When my days were dark, You shed light on my path. When I was burdened and heavy laden, You said, "Come unto me, and I will give you rest." Lord, I know how to take everything to You in prayer. I know that if I trust You and never doubt that You will always bring me out.

Lord, continue to use me as You see fit, I am ready and willing, to do Your will. So prepare situations before me where I would always be tested, situations that would keep me on my knees, oh God, situations that would allow someone else to see what You have done for me, and long to taste and see that the Lord is good. So have thine own way Lord, have thine own way with me.

Ask God to have His own way in your life today and allow Him to do His will.

Singing Praises to God

Show God how important He is in your life; find reasons to praise Him all through the day. I have let this become a habit that I never plan to break. If you begin to thank God for the little blessing in your life, you will find so many reasons to praise God all the daylong. You don't have to be on your knees to praise God; you could be driving in your car, in your garden, or just out walking. Just look around you and you will find something to praise God for.

Lord, I am lifting Your name on high this day. I am singing Your praises all the daylong, because I am nothing without You. You alone know the desires of my heart, and because of Your loving-kindness, goodness and mercy, I can go through each day with a prayer and a praise.

All the daylong I communicate with You. I want to tell the whole world about You. I continually thank You for all that You are doing in my life. I have been through fiery trials, and You have brought me out, so I have reasons to shout. You are worthy to be praised.

Lord, when our praises go up blessings come down. When we find reasons to praise You, You bless us even more. It is always a good thing to give You thanks and praise, always and everywhere.

There is power in our praise. There is healing in our praise. There is joy in our praise.

There is deliverance in our praise, and there is abundance in our praise.

Thank God today for your trials and your pains; praise Him anyway, knowing that He understands.

Living Daily for God

When we meditate on God's Word daily, we grow spiritually. I read my Bible every day for inspiration. No matter what I am going through, when I open my Bible there is always a verse or a Scripture that speaks to my spirit, and that is enough to carry me through the day. When I read the Scriptures, I get a better understanding of God's Word that helps me to grow spiritually.

Blessed is the man whose delight is in the law of the Lord, and who meditates on it day and night. Your Word, oh Lord, will be a light unto his feet, and a lamp unto his path. Knowing this, help me to continue to live daily for You by feasting and meditating on Your Word, so that I may continue to walk in Your marvelous light.

Dear Lord, let me not be like a chafe before the wind, let me not be like the restless wave driven and tossed by the sea. Let me not be a doubtful Thomas who only believes what he sees, but by faith, believe, that with You, all things are possible, that a thousand years in Your sight is like a day to You when it's past, and understand that there is nothing impossible for You.

Lord, I want to obey Your laws. I want to be guided by You. Lord, Your way is right. Your way is perfect. Only let me do what is pleasing in Your sight. Each day, oh Lord, help me to focus on Your Word, living daily for You, fixing my thoughts on You.

Lord, when I am tempted to sin, show me a way out. Lord, give me a heart to praise You always. Use me to be a blessing to others even as You bless me. I want to be able to tell others of Your goodness and mercy, and that because You live, I can face tomorrow. Help me to continue living daily for You, by feasting and meditating on Your Word.

Dear Lord, give me a deeper understanding of Your Word so that I may grow spiritually.

Living a God-Dependent Life

Learn to live by faith and not by sight, depending on God for everything. It took me a long time to understand the real meaning of living a God-Dependent life. I now understand that God already knows the things that I need, so now I just thank Him in advance for the things I need and wait, and I am never disappointed.

Thank You, dear Lord, that because I have learned to live a God-dependent life, I am able to turn pain into praise and heartaches into hallelujahs. Because I am living a God-dependent life, I can put fears to flight. I can trade worries for waiting, and weary for willingness, confident, that all things will work together for my good because I love God.

Thank You dear Lord, that because I am living a God-dependent life, I can praise You more and criticize You less. I can thank You in the midst of my struggles. I can give to others even when I don't have enough for myself. I can bring comfort to others even when my troubles get me down. I can lift You up in praise even after I have been disappointed, and I can thank You for unanswered prayers.

Thank You dear Lord, that because I am living a God-dependent life, I can praise You in good times and in bad times. I can sing from behind prison walls. I can climb mountains with an aching back. I can give to the poor even though I am living in poverty. I could see the good in any bad situation. I could praise You even though I am going through trials, and I know how to thank You for my joys, as well as my strifes.

When I trust God with all of my heart and mind and strength, all things will work together for my good. When I give my best to You, oh Lord, You always make provision for me. When I hope in the Lord, I am never disappointed. When I learned to cast all my cares on You oh Lord, my burdens got easier to bear, and since I have learned to live a God-dependent life I always have enough.

Heavenly Father, show me how to live a God-dependent life.

Thanksgiving

How Can I Forget to Thank You, Lord?

The Lord is good every time, yet we forget so easily the wonderful things He does for us. Sometimes our prayers are answered in such a way that we don't recognize it. There have been times when I prayed for something, and because God did not answer in the way I was expecting, it went unrecognized. I have prayed for God to increase my faith, and my troubles were multiplied. You could be praying for a house, and God will give you an apartment. How we handle what He gives to us will always determine how much more we receive.

How can I forget to thank You, Lord, for the wonderful things You are doing in my life?

How could I ever turn back from serving You, oh Lord? You keep working things out for me. You have made rivers for me in the desert, and You shower me with rain through my dry seasons, and I am so overwhelmed by Your goodness and mercy.

How can I forget to thank You, Lord? You have been holding me up through the storms of life. You give me a heart to praise Your name; You have shown me how to be a beacon for others; to shine light on those I meet and give encouragement to others who are discouraged.

How can I forget to thank You Lord? I know that You are walking with me. I know that You are pleased with me. I know that You did not forget me, because You answered my prayers, and I will continue to serve You with my whole heart. I will never put anything or anyone before You. You have humbled me in ways I could not have imagined, and I am thankful for Your love.

How can I forget to thank You Lord? You are continually watching over me; You are continually searching me and trying me. Lord, I am confident in my Christian life, keep building me up; keep strengthening my walk with You; keep using me for Your glory, and help me never to become complacent in my walk with You.

Lord, I am depending on You to order my steps that I may walk uprightly. I am depending on You to water my garden continually so that others may enjoy my beautiful flowers. I am depending on You to keep me rooted and grounded in You, and to show me how to thank You for all the wonderful things You are doing in my life.

Believe today that God will do something wonderful for you. Just trust Him.

I Will Bless the Lord
at All Times

Bless the Lord at all times and let His praise continually be in your mouth. I could bless the Lord at all times because He is forever giving me reasons to do so. I have experienced in Him fullness of joy, so it is easy for His praises to be always in my mouth.

"I will bless the Lord at all times; His praise shall continually be in my mouth" (Psalm 34:1). Oh, I am so glad, dear Lord, that I know You and have experienced in You fullness of joy. I will lift You up in praise from the rising of the sun, to its setting.

Lord, I am resting in You daily; I am refreshed by You daily; I am Yours, and You are mine; I can claim You because You first claimed me; I can love You because You first loved me.

"Oh, where could I go and You are not there? Oh, what could I do without You not knowing? Or where could I hide that You cannot find me? If I run to the hills You are there; if I run to the sea You are there" (Psalm 139:7–9).

I cannot escape You, oh Lord, and would always want to be under Your watchful eyes and Your guiding hands, being led by You, being comforted by You, and be able to bless and praise You, oh Lord, at all times.

I will lift You up in praise at every turn in my life. You provide situations in my life good and bad that cause me to praise You. I am especially thankful for my trials, for Your love and mercy so freely given, so tender so true.

There is no love like Your love. There is no father as forgiving to His children, as You are. Lord, I will bless You at all times, because without Your guidance I am nothing; without You leading me and guiding me, my destinations would be fruitless,

So I will bless You, oh Lord, at all times. I will enter into Your gates daily with thanksgiving and into Your courts with praise, for You, oh Lord, are good, Your mercy is everlasting and Your truth endures to all generations. Amen.

Gracious Father, please provide situations in my life daily that would give me reasons to praise You.

Prayer for a New Day

We should always give God thanks for the new day and His new mercies promised to us. The Lord watches over us at night when we sleep—many don't wake up. Those of us whom He awakens to enjoy the day that He has given us, let us rejoice and be glad.

"This is the day that the Lord has made; We will rejoice and be glad in it" (Psalm 118:24).

Lord, how wonderful it is to give You thanks on a brand new morning, throughout the day, and again at evening time. Lord, it is because of Your goodness and mercy that I am able to see each new day. Thank You, Lord, for the new mercies and promised blessings that You will bestow on me.

Thank You for restoring me and protecting me through the night. I know, Lord, that today You are leading me to greener pastures. I know dear Lord that You are anointing my head with fresh oil and I believe today that my cup will overflow. Lord, help me never to be ungrateful but always to be thankful. Help me to show mercy to others as You have shown me.

Thank You, dear Lord, for removing from me all doubts and fears, and for the ability to cast all of my cares on You. Lord, I am Your child. You have called me by name. You have put so much gladness in my heart. Today, I will use my gifts and talents for Your glory, and I ask You to bless the fruits of my labor, and in any area that I am lacking. I know that You will provide all that I need today. Thank You, Lord, for Your blessings on me.

God will provide all that I am in need of today.

Oh, That Men Would Praise the Lord

Let us praise God in good times and in bad times. I have praised God when my burdens were heavy, I have praised God when I couldn't find a way out, I have praised God when things were good, and I have praised God when things were bad. When I praised Him in the good times, He blessed me, and when I praised Him in the bad times, He made a way for me. Oh, that men would praise the Lord.

I will sing unto the Lord a new song, for He has done marvelous things. How can I begin to thank You, dear Lord, for the wonderful things that You are doing in my life? What can I do to show You how grateful I am?

Lord, I know that I am not perfect; I know that I am a sinner saved by grace. I know that when I can't pray that You listen to my heart, You intercede for me.

I know that when I am troubled, when I am lost and can't find my way, that I could come boldly before You and You will provide comfort for me.

Lord, when I think of Your goodness and mercy toward me each day, my heart is overwhelmed, and that is when I need You to lead me to the rock that is higher than I.

That is when I need You to hide me under the shadow of Your wings. That is when I need You to divide the Red Sea for me to cross over and escape the enemy.

Oh, that men would praise the Lord for His goodness and His mercy. Oh, that men would give God the praise when their way is dark.

Oh, that men would lift high the name of Jesus for His wonderful acts. Oh, that men would praise the Lord when their burdens are heavy.

Oh, that men would praise the Lord when they have tried and failed. Oh that men would praise the Lord when it seems like there is no way out.

Our God is a forgiving and an understanding God. He knows our needs before we ask them. He has already prepared tables before us in the presence of our enemies.

He has already opened doors for us to walk through. He has already created paths for us to walk in.

So, dear Lord, teach us to cast our cares on You. Teach us to come humbly before You, believing, that You oh God, are all powerful, that You will deliver our Daniel, that You will save us from fires that will consume us, that You will deliver us from our Pharaohs, that You will guide us like Your lost sheep.

Lord, we serve You because You are an awesome God. Open our eyes so that we may behold Your goodness and mercy each day and give You the praise and honor due to Your name. Oh that men would praise the Lord.

I will praise You, oh God, for Your goodness and mercy toward me each and every day.

How Manifold Are
Your Works

Ask God to open your eyes to behold His marvelous works. There is so much beauty all around me, many times when I am feeling down, it's something as simple as the birds singing in my hibiscus tree, or to see a new rose bloom in my garden to lift me up. Whenever you are feeling down, instead of fixing your mind on the problem, open your eyes to behold the beauty of earth.

"Oh Lord, how manifold are Your works! In wisdom You have made them all" (Psalm 104:24). I am so thankful that I am alive to behold Your marvelous works.

There is so much beauty all around me. There is so much to thank You for. Where do I begin?

Lord, Your works are pure; Your works are perfect. When I awake each morning, I see the dawning of the new day, with the rising of the sun in all its glory.

The birds begin to sing. The dew is still wet on the grass. The cool winds blowing in the trees, the sweet fragrance of the blossoms, the buzz of the bees, and then I am reminded, that it was You, oh God, who created the beauty of this earth.

I then break the fast of the night just past, with food that You created for nourishing our bodies, and from the rising of the sun to its setting, I am overwhelmed by Your awesome works.

At evening time, after the sun begins to shine its light on another part of this beautiful earth, You light the evening skies with the moon and the stars, another reminder, that You are watching over us day and night, oh Lord, how marvelous are Your works.

You have done so many wonderful things, and each day, You reveal Your Glory and bless us with Your mercy and grace. How can we ever forget, oh Lord? How manifold are Your works.

Open my eyes today oh, Lord, to behold Your marvelous works.

I Am Blessed
Beyond Measure

Count your many blessings, and be thankful for them. God is the giver of all good things. God has blessed me so much. I try to recount my blessings in order but cannot. Look around you, when you see what others are going through, count your many blessings.

All that I have is blessed because I trusted in You, oh Lord. Everything around me is blessed. I cannot number my blessings in order.

My home is blessed. My dreams are blessed. My finances are blessed. My obligations are blessed. My situations are blessed. My career is blessed.

My achievements are blessed. My crops are blessed. My troubles are blessed, and my trials that make me stronger are blessed.

Lord, You have been my support. "You brought me out into a broad place. You delivered me because you delighted in me" (Psalm 18:19). "Your thoughts are precious towards me," (Psalm 139:17) and that is why I am so very blessed.

My health is blessed. My heart is blessed. My offerings are blessed. My spirit is blessed. My way is blessed.

My circumstances are blessed. My labor is blessed. My salvation is blessed. My hope is blessed, and my trust in You, oh Lord, is blessed.

"Lord, my goodness is nothing apart from You…The lines have fallen unto me in pleasant places" (Psalm 16:2,6).

Lord, because of You I have a good inheritance, and that is why my parents are blessed. My grandparents are blessed. My children are blessed. My grandchildren are blessed. My brothers and sisters are blessed.

My uncles are blessed. My aunts are blessed. My nieces are blessed. My nephews are blessed. My marriage is blessed. All of my relationships are blessed.

Thank You, Lord, for blessing me beyond measure. I cannot remember my blessings in order nor am I able to count them.

When You bless me so much, oh God, show me how to be a blessing to others.

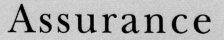

Assurance

An Opening Prayer

I begin and end each day with prayer. I give God thanks in the morning and again at evening time for each and every new day.

Heavenly Father, we are thankful for this new day that You have made, we will rejoice and be glad in it. Lord, we know that we are here today, not because of anything good that we have done, but because of Your unending goodness and mercy. We come boldly before You this day, with prayerful and thankful hearts. We know not what this day will bring forth, but we are trusting You for good things.

Dear God, every day we are faced with new challenges, but You have not left us defenseless. You have made us fit for battle, so help us to put on the whole armor of God so that we would be ready to stand, not in our own might, but in Your strength. Help us to understand that our challenges would help us to grow, and show us how to use them as stepping stones and not stumbling blocks.

Lord, Your Word reminds us that where two and three are gathered in Your name, that You are in the midst, and we bring before You this morning, all those who are sick, who are troubled, who have lost loved ones, who are in need, who are suffering with addictions, and we ask that You deliver, restore, comfort, and heal them, and for those who could not be here with us today for whatever reason, reach out and bless them in special ways.

Lord, You have been watching over us; You have been protecting us; You did not let our enemies triumph over us, You have fed us when we were hungry, and You have turned our sorrows into joy. We know that we could depend on You for comfort, for healing, for restoration and deliverance; and we pray that the words of our mouths, and the meditations of our hearts, would always be acceptable in Your sight. Amen.

"This is the day that the Lord has made, I will rejoice and be glad in it" (Psalm 118:24).

Waiting on the Lord

Waiting for anything is hard, but waiting on the Lord sometimes seems even harder. Trust in the Lord and wait patiently on Him. For me, waiting on the Lord is work in progress, but as I grow spiritually, waiting faithfully on the Lord becomes easier. We get frustrated waiting, because we cannot see ahead, but we must understand that "faith is the substance of things hoped for and the evidence of things not seen" (Hebrews 11:1). God may be telling you to wait because of what He knows is ahead.

I have been trusting You oh God, for good things. I have been waiting on You to answer my prayers. I keep losing my way, but Lord, I am still here.

What is it that You require of me? Show me what You want me to do. Lord, I have been brought so low. My back is against the wall.

I don't know where to turn. I don't know what to do, so I will continue to trust You. I will continue to wait on You oh Lord and be of good courage, knowing that You will strengthen my heart.

Lord, I have been down and out before, and You brought me out, and I am confident that You will bring me out again, that You will make a way for me, that You are working Your purpose out for me.

When I am down oh Lord, I could only look up to You, when I lose my way oh Lord, I could only reach out to You and trust You to come to my aide.

Lord, I have strived to walk in Your ways. I have been striving to do Your will, and because I know that I serve a living and an understanding God, I will wait on You because You are the same God yesterday, today, and forever.

I will continue to praise You in the midst of this struggle, I will continue to be strong in the faith, confident that this too shall pass.

Lord, Your Word reminds me that no shame will come upon me whilst I wait on You, that "You will pluck my feet out of this net" (Psalm 25:15). You will bring me out victorious. I will be the victor and not the victim in this situation.

So thank You, Lord, for this assurance. I will wait patiently on You, the author and finisher of my faith. Not my will, oh Lord, but Thy will be done. Amen.

Lord, I cannot see what lies ahead, but I will trust You.

You Carried Me

God will carry you when you are too tired to walk. There are many times when I have been so tired, so overwhelmed that I wished for someone to pick me up, and God did; He carried me when I was too tired to walk. Your journey may not be long, but you could get tired easily just carrying your troubles. God is always ready to take your yoke upon Him and carry you, when you are too tired to walk.

Thank You, Lord, for carrying me when I was too tired to walk, thank You Lord, that You did not give up on me, when I had given up on myself.

Thank You Lord, that I was being guided by Your footprints in the sand, thank You, Lord, that I kept holding on to Your unchanging hand.

Thank You Lord, that even though I was down and out, You gave me a reason to sing and a reason to shout.

Now I know that where I am is where You want me to be. I know that where I am going You are leading me.

Lord, I have been through the fire. I have been through storms. I have felt pain and heartaches, and I have known want and need.

I have been distressed and downtrodden; I was ridiculed and abused, but thank You, Lord, for where I am now. Thank You, Lord, for where You are leading me.

Now my pastures are green, I feed on food I have not prepared; help comes to me in my darkest hour, from sources that I can't explain.

My prayers are answered, my health is restored, my body is refreshed, my heart is at ease, because I trusted You oh Lord, for everything, I prayed to You, oh Lord, about everything.

Now, I am drinking from the fountain, I've changed the saucer to a bowl, my water has been turned into wine, my tears into laughter and my sight has been restored. I am walking in the light of the Lord.

I am now able to say, come, and sit down, let me tell You me about my awesome God; Let me tell you from whence my healing streams doth flow; Let me tell you where my strength comes from; Let me tell you who holds me up when I am weak; Let me tell you who carries me when I am too tired to walk.

Thank You, Lord, for carrying me when I am too tired to walk.

Yet, I Will Rejoice
in the Lord

Rejoice in the Lord, no matter what your situation may be. I have found myself in situations where I have seen others in the same situation fall apart, but I find myself rejoicing in the Lord. I don't know how my bills are going to be paid, but I am writing the checks in faith.

"Though the fig tree may not blossom, nor fruit be on the vines: Though the labor of the olive may fail, and the fields yield no food: Though the flock may be cut off from the fold and there be no herd in the stalls—Yet, I will rejoice in the Lord" (Habakkuk 3:17–18).

Oh, how good and pleasant it is to rejoice in the Lord despite your situation. Lord, my strength fails, yet, I will rejoice in You. My heart is pained, yet, I will rejoice in You. Lord, I know not where my next meal will come from or how I will pay my bills, yet, I will rejoice in the Lord.

My friends have turned against me; I am in trouble and there is none to help, yet, I will rejoice in the Lord. The doctors have given up hope for my health problems, my spirit is crushed; I am groaning in pain all the day long, yet, I will rejoice in the Lord.

Because I believe in Your Word, oh Lord, that weeping may endure for a night or two, but joy will come in the morning, that they that wait upon the Lord shall renew their strength, that they who trust in You oh Lord, will not lack anything good, and, therefore, no matter what my situation, I will rejoice in You. Amen.

I will rejoice in You oh Lord, despite of what I am in need of today.

Repentance
and
Forgiveness

Come Boldly Before the Lord

No matter what we have done, God reminds us that we can come to Him in prayer and seek forgiveness. Just as God wants us to be specific in our prayers, He wants us to confess our sins in the same manner.

Thank You, dear Lord that I could come before Your presence boldly, no matter what I have done. Lord, my thoughts and actions have not been perfect; I have followed too much the desires of my own heart, but thank You, dear Lord, that I have learned to make my prayers to You, a vital part of all of my days.

Thank You, dear Lord, for the confidence in knowing that even though I have been weak and sinful and vile, that I could still make my requests known to You. Dear Lord, You have assured me that You hear us when we pray; You have assured me that You answer every prayer when we ask, seek, and knock.

But, Lord, there have been times when I have prayed and I kept on praying, and it seemed like You had forgotten me, but I am thankful, dear Lord, that I was steadfast in my prayer, that I was earnest and vigilant and persistent.

I know, dear Lord, that if You delayed in answering my prayers that it was for my own good. I know, dear Lord, that You are an on-time God. Maybe, dear Lord, I have been disobedient, rebellious, unforgiving, selfish, and have followed too much the devices of my own heart. If there is anything, anything in my life that I cannot see because of my blindness, I am asking You Lord, please remove it.

Forgive me for all the wrongs that I have done; humble me, oh God, give me the wisdom and courage and patience to wait on You. Take me to the point, dear Lord, where I can bring all of my burdens to You, that I can lift my prayers up to You, and spiritually position me, so that I could accept Your blessings and trust You completely for the right answer at the right time. In Jesus' name I pray. Amen.

Today I will confess my sins to You, oh God, and I ask Your forgiveness.

Keep Your Mind Fixed on the Lord

When you are praying and your mind is wandering, ask God to forgive you and to keep you focused.

Heavenly Father, my mind is wandering when it should be fixed on You. I am not focused on You as I should be. I have not been diligent in prayer as I should. I have not been meditating on Your Word as I should, forgive me dear Lord.

Lord, I do not want anything or anyone to come before You, so clear my mind, oh God, to refocus my thoughts on You, to do the things You need me to do. If I have put anything or anyone before You, forgive me dear Lord.

Lord, I want to fix my mind on heavenly things. I want to think Your thoughts. I want to be an example for others. I want my words to be gentle and kind. If I have sinned in thought, word or deed, if I have been unkind to anyone, forgive me dear Lord.

I want to conduct myself in way that is pleasing to You. I want to live my life in such a way, so that others will see Christ in me. If my way has not been pleasing to You, if I have not lived the life I sing about, forgive me dear Lord.

Lord, when I come before Your presence I want to do so humbly. I want to be able to be in Your presence, reflecting on You, listening to You. If I have come before You in anger or arrogance, forgive me dear Lord.

Lord, I do not only want to be able to bring my troubles to You, but to seek Your will for my life, to seek direction from You and to pray for guidance as I walk with You. If I have followed the devices of my heart excessively, forgive me dear Lord.

The next time I come into Your presence and my mind is not totally fixed on You, search my mind, see if anything is there that should not be and remove it. I want to be able to hear Your still, small voice, and understand Your directions, and be prepared to carry out the good works that You have prepared for me to do.

Today, I am praying and my mind keeps wandering, clear my mind, oh God, to stay focused on You.

A Prayer for Forgiveness

God is more willing to hear us than we are to pray and ask for forgiveness. If we confess our sins, God is faithful and just and will forgive us from all unrighteousness.

Oh, God, You are a forgiving and an understanding God. You are more willing to hear us than we are to pray; and so, dear God, I confess that I have sinned against thee. I am not worthy; I am not worthy; I am not worthy. But I know You have the power to save and to set free.

Lord, Your Word reminds us that "if we say we have no sin, we deceive ourselves and the truth is not in us" (John 1:8), but if we confess our sins that You are faithful and just and will forgive us from all unrighteousness. So I will not be a liar, I will confess my sins to You today oh Lord, and ask Your forgiveness.

Lord, I have done things that I am ashamed of. I have uttered words that I cannot take back. I have grieved Your Holy Spirit; I have grieved Your Holy Spirit, and I need Your forgiveness.

This old heart of mine is burdened. I am unable to look at myself in the mirror. My friends have turned away from me. I am drowning daily in my sorrows. Revive me; revive me, dear Lord.

Lord, I have been high, and I have been brought so low. Because of my sins, I feel like my life is no longer my own. So I am giving it back to You; I am giving it back to You, confident, that You can make all things new.

Lord, I am a broken vessel. I am battered and bruised. I am driven and tossed like the waves of the sea. I called and no one answered; I called out and no one answered, but hear oh Lord, and answer me. Hear my prayer and forgive me.

Dear Lord, I have been a slave to sin for far too long. Please set this captive free.

Holding on against God's Will

What are we struggling to hold on to? What is separating us from God's love? We must learn to let go and let God take control. This does not mean to let go at the first sign of trouble, but there are times when we take possession of things, we make our plans before first making our requests known to God and seeking His will. As a result, many times these become barriers that are blocking our true blessings.

Dear God, I have so many questions that I know only You can answer; only You could give me the direction and guidance I need at this time. I need to know if I am holding on against Your will.

It's dear to my heart; I love it so much, but is it God's will for my life? Is this a blessing or a barrier in my life? Am I holding on against God's will?

I am struggling to hold on to things no matter what the price. I am holding on to things that cause me so much pain, and never any gain.

I am holding on to relationships, past hurts, my dreams, jobs, houses, businesses and so much more.

Lord, I am struggling to hold on to everything, it is taking all that I have to give, they are becoming too burdensome to keep, I am doing the very things I know that I should not do.

I am now wondering if I am holding on against Your will. How and when would I recognize that I am holding on against Your will?

Heavenly Father, Your Word reminds me, that anything that separates me from Your love is surely against Your will.

Anything that causes me to sin is definitely against Your will. My sins have hidden Your face from me so You do not hear me when I call.

So I am now confident oh God, that I have been going against Your will just to hold on to relationships, jobs, houses, businesses and so much more.

I desire these more than You oh God, they have become an idol in my heart. I put them before You oh God. Please forgive me.

I will learn to let go of my sinful desires, these barriers that have been blocking my blessings and let You oh God take control.

I know oh God, that You will never close one door, unless You have another prepared. I know that You have a plan and a purpose for my life.

I will allow You oh God to work Your purpose out for my life. If I learn to desire You only oh God, I know that I will be able to distinguish the difference between the blessings from the barriers in my life, and nothing will ever again separate me from Your love. Amen.

Dear God, I pledge today to make all of my requests known to You and await Your direction and allow nothing to separate me from Your love.

Encouragement

A Prayer of Reflection

Through prayer and reflection we could see how we are growing Spiritually. We could examine ourselves to determine our hindrances to God's blessings and seek His guidance in going forward.

This year has been trying for us in so many different ways, but through it all we have made it this far, not on our own merits, but through Christ who strengthens us.

Let us remember, that God gives us more grace when the burdens grow greater, and He sends more help when the labor increases. So let us learn to trust God for everything, and with prayer and supplication give Him thanks always.

In these trying times, it is easy for us to become selfish and think of our own needs. It is so easy to turn away from helping those in need. But help us, dear Lord, not to focus on our situations, but instead to extend ourselves to the good of others.

In these trying times, we should ask ourselves these questions: What is my focus? What are my goals? Am I on the construction gang or the wrecking crew? Am I building others up or tearing them down?

No matter how difficult times are for you, if you learn to smooth the path for others, God will smooth the path for you. When you put stumbling blocks in the paths of others, how can you expect God to make your path straight? You cannot block blessings from others and expect God to bless you.

God loves a cheerful giver. Learn to give and to lend a helping hand without expecting anything in return. I am so thankful, dear Lord that I am striving daily to walk in Your ways. I am so glad that I have learned the secret to living a God-dependent life.

There are others who are quick to judge you, who believe that all is well with you because they never hear you complain. They never see you when your back is against the wall.

But when you learn to live a God-dependent life, you will find that it becomes easier to say, "Thank You, God," in the midst of your trials. You will learn to praise God more and criticize Him less.

As I reflect on the year just past, it affords me the opportunity to remember all those who have been there for me; all those whose prayers, support, and encouragement throughout the year have helped me through difficult times.

We don't see each other as often as we would like, but let us continue to lift each other up in our daily prayers, and most importantly, faith without works is dead, so lend a hand, share, and comfort each other. Let us learn to bear each other's burden, just as Christ did for us. Amen.

Today, I will thank You, dear Lord, for the things I have and trust You for what I need.

Delight Yourself
in the Lord

If the Lord is delighted in you, He will give you the desires of your heart. When I fully committed myself to the Lord, I began to experience His blessings in every area of my life. I believe also that my best is yet to come. God wants us to commit to Him fully, and He has promised that if we do, we will not lack anything good.

"Delight yourself in the Lord, and He will give you the desires of your heart. Commit your way to the Lord" (Psalm 37:4–5), and He will make your path straight. Ask for God's guidance in all that you do. Lean not unto your own understanding, but seek His will for your life through prayer, so that you may be pleasing to Him." Humble yourself before the Lord.

When you fully commit yourself to the Lord, you will lack nothing that is good. He will order your steps, and even though you go through the fire, you will not be burned. He will satisfy your needs in parched places. He will protect you from every fiery dart of the wicked. He will fill your life with good things.

In all your ways acknowledge Him and He will direct your path. You are reminded through Scripture, that God is able to bless you abundantly, so that in all things and at all times, having all that you need and that you will abound in every good work.

When others are being blessed around you, don't be jealous or angry. Wait on the Lord. As long as you continue to trust Him with all your heart, you could say with confidence, "I am next in line for my blessing."

When you see others around you who are being blessed, recognize that blessings come from God in His own timing. So, keep holding on to God's unchanging hand. Keep your eye on the prize—Heaven, look to God who is the author and finisher of your faith. He makes all things come to pass.

God has not forgotten you. He will put a song in your heart when the tune is right. He will send floodwaters when the river is high. He will break branches when they are heavy with fruit. He will bring forth light where there is darkness. He will restore your strength when you are weak. He will give birth after labor pains. So "Delight yourself in the Lord, and He will give you the desires of your heart" (Psalm 37:4). Amen.

Today, I will commit my life to You, oh God. I want You to bless me in every area of my life.

Is There Anything Too Hard for God?

Understand that there is no problem, situation, or circumstance greater than God. I know that there is nothing too hard for my God, because He has made things possible for me when I was only able to see the impossible. Let God handle all of your problems, situations, or circumstances that seem impossible.

Heavenly Father, I am facing a situation this morning that seems impossible. Remind me, remind me dear Lord, that I am seeing the impossible, but that You will do the impossible. As I go through this day, remind me of the many times You have done the impossible. So I will ask myself when I am tempted to doubt Your abilities…

Is there anything too hard for my God? The same miracle-working God we know, the same God who parted the Red Sea, the same God who delivered Daniel from the lion's den, the same God who turned water into wine?

Is there anything too hard for my God? The same God who restored sight to the blind, who made the lame to walk, the dumb to talk, the same God who raised the dead to life again?

Is there anything too hard for my God? The same God who created the seasons of change, who caused the sun to shine by day, and the moon to shine by night and showers the earth with rain when it is dry?

Is there anything too hard for my God? My God who is the same yesterday, today, and forever? The same God who provided manna for His children, the same God who brought forth water from a rock, who caused the sun to stand still?

Is there anything too hard for my God? The same God who created the earth and sky and all the creatures in it, divided the night from the day, and separated the sea from dry land, the same God who created You?

Thank You dear Lord, that I believe in my heart, that there is absolutely nothing too hard for You. Man sees the impossible, but You could do the impossible.

I will lay all of my burdens at Your feet today, dear Lord, confident that You will be my burden bearer.

Don't Give Up

If only we could see how close we are to our breakthroughs, we would hold on to God's unchanging hand. I know that I have given up too soon before, all because I was not able to see how close to my breakthrough I was. But I have also learned to persevere. I did not give up when the going got rough, and God has rewarded me double for my trouble.

Many times I have prayed and did not get an answer. Many times I was in need and didn't know where to turn. I was in prison, and no one came to rescue me. I was sick and no one came to visit me. My spirit was crushed my strength was weak, but I did not give up.

I did not know how to face my tomorrow, because I was struggling to get through today. I was afraid to pray because my answers were delayed. I could not sing because my heart was pained, but I did not give up.

Problems assailed me from every side. My burdens got heavier at every turn. I was accused, and ridiculed, I was scorned and oppressed. I was tempted and tried, but I did not give up.

I felt lost and alone. No one reached out to comfort me. I was battered and bruised and no one seemed to care. I was hungry, and no one invited me to eat, but I did not give up.

Because, deep in my heart I believed, deep in my heart I trusted, deep in my heart I was convinced, that the God that I served, said, "This too shall pass."

Now I am rejoicing for my strength has been renewed. Now I am telling others, that because I did not give up, because I did not give in, the desires of my heart are being fulfilled.

Lord, give me the strength I need today to hold on to You in prayer and not give up too soon.

Give It over to God

When you have tried everything and have failed, give it over to God. He could make all things new. We cannot accomplish anything through our own strength, but many times we believe that we could do it on our own. When we find that we have done all that we could and we are still not succeeding, we should always give it over to God, thus acknowledging that He is all powerful and that He cannot fail.

Holy and gracious Father, earth has no sin or sorrow that You in heaven cannot bear, and because I am aware of this, I am burdened and heavy laden and I am giving it over to You, all of my troubles and trials that I cannot seem to bear.

When I have tried, when I have done all that I could, when I have prayed, and it seems like my prayers are being unanswered, I will give it over to You oh God.

When I am in trouble and there is no one to help, when I am sick and doctors have given up hope, when I have hit rock bottom with no way up, I will give it over to You, oh God.

When I am overburdened, when I am heavy laden, when I am refused and abused, when I have fallen and can't get up, when I am downtrodden, I will give it over to God.

I am believing today, that when I give it over to You oh God, that I am acknowledging Your power, Your forgiveness, and Your love for me, that I know You are slow to anger and endless in mercy.

When I give it over to You oh God, I am trusting You to do the impossible. When I give it over to You oh God, I am expecting healing, deliverance and an answer to my prayers.

When I give it over to You oh God, I am believing You for a breakthrough. When I give it over to You oh God, it means that I am admitting that I have depended on my own strength, and that I have tried and have failed.

When I give it over to You oh God, I am accepting that I can do nothing on my own strength. Therefore, I will give it over to You; sit patiently and wait for You to act.

Holy and gracious Father, I acknowledge today that I could accomplish nothing in my own strength, so I will give it over to You, the author and finisher of my faith.

Everything to God in Prayer

We must learn to take everything to God in prayer, no matter how small the trouble or situation may be. I have prayed for my lawn when the chinch bugs attacked and when God answered by restoring my lawn I was so very thankful. There is no prayer too insignificant for God to hear.

Everything to God in prayer; I mean *everything* to God in prayer; Take *everything* to God in prayer.

When your children don't listen; when the lawn mower stops working; when the bills are unpaid; take it to God in prayer.

Your mother is sick, your friend borrows and does not repay, your neighbor is causing you pain, take it to God in prayer.

You need a new job, you car is on its last journey, you need a place to live, take it to God in prayer.

When you are facing so much, remember, that the Lord is your shepherd and you shall not want. He will make you lie down in green pastures. He will lead you beside still waters. He will restore your soul.

He will prepare a table before you in the presence of your enemies. He will anoint your head with oil, and your cup will overflow. He will not lead you into temptation, and He will deliver you from all evil (Psalm 23).

So no matter what you need, no matter what the problem is, no matter what your situation, no matter what the circumstance, learn to take *everything* to God in prayer.

I will begin today to take everything to You, oh God, in prayer.

Jesus Is the Answer

We must turn our eyes upon Jesus for all the answers to our problems. Some of us are known as Jacks of all trades and masters of none; we look for quick fixes to our problems. But I know that God is the ultimate problem solver. He is the God of completion, so let us look to Him for all the answers to our problems.

You have questions. You have problems. You have a decision to make. You are worried. You are sick in mind, body, and spirit. What is the solution to all this? Who alone can understand all this? Who alone can see you through this? Jesus is the answer.

When your husband or wife fails you, when your children have turned against you, when your brother is angry with you, when your loved one is suddenly taken from you, who alone can see you through all this? Jesus is the answer.

When you are discouraged, feeling lost and alone, when your friends have let you down, when enemies confront you from every side; who alone can see you through all this? Jesus is the answer.

Jesus is the ultimate problem solver, burden bearer, protector, deliverer, comforter, healer, helper, and friend. He is our rock and our strength, our Jehovah Jireh. Jesus is the answer.

Thank You, Lord, for the assurance that You will provide the answers that I need today.

A Light in the Darkness

When we are down and out, when our way seems dark, we must look to Jesus. He is our light in the darkness. I used to believe that my only darkness could be when the light bulb is blown or when the sun goes down. I thought that by replacing the light bulb or waiting for the dawn, were the only source of my light in the darkness. I have been in dark places in my life, I have experienced darkness in my life, which required a more powerful light, and I found it in Jesus, the light of the world. When you have this light on the inside, Jesus wants you to share it with others, so that they may see and know that He is the light, which is life.

"I will arise and shine, for my light has come, and the Glory of the Lord is risen upon me" (Isaiah 60:1). When my way is dark, I could rest assured that *Jesus* will be my light in the darkness. I have turned many dark corners in my life, but *Jesus* has been my light in my darkest hour.

He refreshed my soul when my spirit was crushed; when I was bowed down He lifted me up; when I was drowning in sorrows He rescued me; He forgave me of all my sins, *Jesus* has been my light in the darkness.

When my child was sick; when my cupboard was bare; when I needed a job; when I had nowhere else to turn; when I needed to hear someone say, it's going to be alright, *Jesus* has been my light in the darkness.

When I needed someone to listen to me, to hear me when I prayed; when I needed a father's loving arms to hold and comfort me; when all my friends turned against me, *Jesus* has been my light in the darkness.

Jesus is the light of the world. His Word reminds me, that "He who follows Him will never walk in darkness, but will have the light, which is life" (John 8:12).

Thank You, dear Lord, that I could depend on You, to be my light in my darkest hours. I could arise and shine, knowing that my light has come and the Glory of the Lord is risen upon me.

Thank You, Jesus, for being my light in my darkest hours.

Peace and Calm

Prayer for Calm

God's calming Spirit could get you through the day. As a Christian, people expect you to be always calm and in control. We try to be, but we are human and are not perfect. The only one who is perfect is God. As Christians, situations arise; they come upon you so unexpectedly, that if you don't immediately stop and ask God to intervene, ask Him for His calming spirit, you could find yourself in a bad place. Every day ask God to shower you with His Grace.

Most holy and gracious Father, I come into your presence this morning with a troubled and angry spirit. I need your calming spirit to help me to get through this day.

Lord, there is no reason for me to be upset over material things. Lord, you have blessed me with this day, and you have showered me with good things.

So why am I rebellious, angry, and grieving Your Holy Spirit? Lord, help me to put off the old man with his deeds. Remind me that I am a new creation.

Lord, Your Word says that we sin by thought, word and deed, so help me to put aside all ungodly thoughts and actions and lead me up and out of this angry state.

I am asking your forgiveness for my unruly thoughts, for my rebellious behavior and for grieving Your Holy Spirit.

Help me to put on the helmet of salvation. Show me how to put on the breastplate of righteousness. Guide me into putting on the sandals of peace.

Bless me with the sword of the spirit, and arm me with Your Holy Word, so that I may be clothed with righteousness and peace until calm returns to me. Amen.

Dear God, please cover me with Your calming spirit today. Send Your guarding angels before me.

Prayer for When You Are Overwhelmed

There are times when everything seems to go wrong at the same time, but the Holy Spirit is able to intercede for us when we are unable. God will sustain you through difficult times. Sometimes, we take on too much too soon; sometimes it's others who entrust us with too much at once. Learn to take every day one day at a time.

I know that when I can't pray, oh Lord, that You listen to my heart. When my troubles overwhelm me, and I can't find words to express my thoughts, imprison me in Your presence and help me to wait for You to act. Lord, Your Word reminds us, that Your Holy Spirit intercedes for us at such times when we are so burdened that words fail us.

Lord, today, You know what I am facing. You alone know what I need to get through this day, so I am asking You to show me where and when to reach out, which door to walk through, and which door to keep closed, and which door to close that I have kept open.

Lord, I have seen my share of troubles, I have suffered so much, but still I am able to thank You for sustaining me through the difficult times. I am confident, that You did not bring me this far to let me go.

I am confident, that all that I have been through, one day I will be able to look back and thank You for my troubles. So I am asking You oh Lord, to give me the strength to do every day what I have to do, and help me to take every day one step at a time.

Lord, teach me to meekly wait and murmur not. Take this anxiety away from me. Lord Your word reminds me to be anxious for nothing, but with prayer and supplication and with thanksgiving, to make my requests known to You.

So, even as I am overwhelmed, continue to move in me to do what is good and right in Your sight, strengthen my faith in You, so that I may endure, knowing that one day I will remember my troubles no more.

Lord, I am trusting You for good things; I am believing You for great things; I am expecting miracles today; and if I pray amiss; if I fail to ask for the right gifts; You know my needs oh Lord, and the good things, which I dare not, or in my blindness cannot ask, I know that You will grant them, oh Father, for Jesus Christ's sake. Amen.

Dear God, I need Your Holy Spirit to intercede on my behalf today as I am overwhelmed by my troubles.

Humility

My Daily Prayer

Daily make your requests known to God, He is ready, willing and able to hear and answer your prayers. Make it a habit to spend quality time with God in prayer. Learn to not only bring your troubles to Him, but to lift Him up in praise and to sit quietly and listen to His voice.

Dear God, we acknowledge that we are inadequate, that we are weak, that we are sinful, and we come humbly before You today, asking You to make whatever adjustments necessary in our lives, so that we could perform such good works as Thou has prepared for us to do.

Dear God, You said, "Your grace is sufficient" (2 Corinthians 12:9). Your Word tells us that "We can do all things through Christ who strengthens us," (Phillipians 4:13) and whatever we are unable to accomplish because of our inadequacies, we know that You, oh God, are able to do more than we could ever ask or deserve.

So, dear God, use us to do Your will, let our conduct and our conversations be compatible with our character, enabling us to be the vessels through which we could attract those who are yet to know You, as the Lord and Master of their lives.

Help us, dear God to walk in Your ways. Oh, the joys of those who love and trust the Lord. Help us, oh God, to take a bold stand for You each day; let us never be afraid or ashamed to tell the whole world what You have done for us.

We are so thankful, dear God that we have learned to wait patiently on You; we are so glad that we have learned to be still in Your presence. Oh, the joys of praising God in the midst of your struggles.

Teach us, oh God, to seek Your will in all we do so that You could direct our paths. Help us to recognize, oh God, that our lives are not our own, and that You will guide us along the best pathways for our lives.

Let Your Word, oh Lord, be a light unto our feet and a lamp unto our paths as You lead and guide us. Give us Your wisdom, oh God, so that we could listen to Your still, small voice, in order to make the right choices.

Move in our hearts to be a blessing to others, as You have blessed us; let our lights shine before others so that they may see Your good works and glorify You. Let us serve You by serving others.

Dear Lord, we are a generation that is always asking You for one thing or the other, but Your Word reminds us "that to whom much is given, much is required" (Luke 12:48). Show us what You want us to do, oh God, and help us to stand ready to Your call. Remove every stumbling block from our lives, oh God that is holding back our blessings.

Teach us to be specific in our prayer. Help us to remain vigilant in prayer. Remind us to remain earnest in prayer, and above all to be persistent in prayer, because our God is an on-time God; He answers every prayer when we ask, seek, and knock. So help us to keep on asking, keep on seeking, and keep on knocking, confident, that God will provide the right answer at the right time. In Jesus' holy name I pray, Amen.

Lord, teach me how to pray aright as I make my requests known to You today.

Praying through Troubled Times

The Lord wants us to come to Him, not only when things are going wrong, but especially when things are good. The Lord will not deal with us as we deserve. He is merciful and will have pity on us. Let us just ask Him to keep providing situations in our lives that would keep us on our knees in prayer and closer to Him. When things are good we tend to forget God until the next time we are faced with a situation and need His help.

Lord, today my burden is heavy, I have no one else to turn to, I don't know where to go, so I am crying out to You for help, do not deal with me as I deserve, have pity on me oh merciful Father. Hear my prayer oh Lord, and let my cry come unto You.

Lord, I need to submit myself totally to You. I need to resist the devil, so that he will flee from me. Lord, You have been with me through the good times, and I know that You will be with me through this bad time.

Lord, You are my strong tower, my rock and my defender. I know that You are able to see me through whatever problems I am facing. You promise never to leave me nor forsake me, and I need You at this time, oh Lord, please do not forsake me now.

Lord, I am crying out to You at this time because I am in great trouble. I did not cry out to You when all was well, but I am thankful, that because of my troubles I can turn to You. I can call on You and trust You to come to my aid, because You are a wonderful, forgiving and merciful God.

Lord I believe, that any problem, situation, or circumstance that brings me to my knees before You, is good for me because when things were good, it was so easy for me to go through life forgetting how to pray.

There were times when I went through life forgetting to thank You, who spread good tables before me; I forgot my Creator who opened doors for me to walk through, who brought me out of many troubles.

I know oh God, that You are a jealous God, and that the same God who spread good tables before me could allow me to suffer want. The same God who opened doors for me could close them, not to hurt me, but to remind me, that all that I am, all that I have, or all that I ever hope to be, I owe it to the glory of God.

Dear God, please do not reward me as I deserve, but be gracious unto me.

My Times Are in Your Hands

Everything we do or say is under God's control. Sometimes, He allows us to believe that we are the ones in control, but then He always has a way to show us that He is the one in control. As the Scripture reminds us, "A man's heart plans His way, but God directs His steps" (Proverbs 16:9).

My times are in Your hands, oh Lord. I know now that You are in control of my life. I will be of good courage, so that You will strengthen my heart, I will continue to hope and trust in You. I will not be afraid.

My times are in Your hands, oh Lord, so I will not fear. I am prepared now to listen to Your voice. Show me where You want me to go. Lead me in the right paths. I will continue to be led by Your guiding hand.

My times are in Your hands, oh Lord, so I know that am I protected. I know now that You will not give me more than I can bear. You will not cause me to suffer long. You will provide peace for me in this storm.

My times are in Your hands, oh Lord, so I will no longer follow the desires of my own heart. I will continue to wait on You all the daylong. Provide comfort for me and anoint my head with fresh oil, so that my cup will overflow.

Lord, I know now, that because my times are in Your hands. I can run and not be weary. I can jump over walls.

I can go through the fire and not be burned, and though my enemies encamp around me, I will be safe.

Lord, my times are in Your hands, I will continue to look to You for direction, because You are my portion and my cup, my strong deliver and my defender. You are all I need. My times are in Your hands oh Lord, so I will not fear.

Lord, please take back control of my life. I have tried to plan my way, but I keep getting lost, please direct my steps.

Confronting Our Weaknesses

We must learn to confront our weaknesses rather than avoid them. We are able to overcome with God's help. I have avoided my weaknesses in the past because I was afraid of confronting them. I ran away from conflict, commitment, challenge, and so much more, until I one day, when I was backed into a corner. It was then I realized that fear is a demon and that God can cast away demons, so I turned to God for deliverance.

Heavenly Father, I am faced with situations in my life which arise from my weaknesses. You know Lord that I have tried to avoid the difficulties, but because I am afraid, because my faith wavers, and my strength fails I am unable to confront them as I should.

I am afraid of my fears and conflict. I am afraid of dealing with feelings of rejection and showing affection to people who are different from me.

I am afraid of stepping out in faith, following my dreams, managing my finances, or just the possibility of change.

I am worried about my future, facing tomorrow, not having enough, or just not trusting You for anything.

Lord, remove doubt, fear, and insecurity from within me. I know that if I am doubtful that I am like the waves, driven and tossed about by the sea.

I also know that if I have faith as small as a grain of mustard seed, I could move mountains, and do all things through Christ who strengthens me.

Lord, help me to understand that "faith is the substance of things hoped for, and the evidence of things not seen," (Hebrews 11:1) and that You will grant me the assurance, so that I could hope for the results I cannot see.

Dear Lord, I want to learn to cast all of my cares on You. I know that I am weak in some areas of my life. I want my weaknesses to be of the past. I want to confront my weaknesses without fear of the unknown outcomes.

I know that when I am afraid, my strength fails, but Your Word reminds me, that even when I am weak, You are strong. So the next time I am facing one of my fears, help me to stand up strong, knowing that Your grace is sufficient for me, that You are my strength and power, and that You will help me to face my fears with confidence.

Holy Father, I am afraid of confronting a weakness in my life today. Please show me how to overcome.

Boast in the Lord

All that we are, all that we have, all that we will be, we owe it to the glory of God. Many of us have good jobs, nice homes, healthy children, and lots of money in the bank that we claim are ours; we forget that we are only the caretakers appointed by God, and that we should thank Him for the opportunity and not boast in ourselves.

"Oh Lord, I know the way of man is not in Himself. It is not in man who walks to direct His own steps. Oh Lord, correct me, but with justice, not in Your anger, lest You bring me to nothing" (Jeremiah 10:23–24).

"But You, oh Lord, know me, You have seen me, You have tested me toward You . . . If you run with footmen and they tire you, then how can you contend with horses?" (Jeremiah 12:3, 5). I could not and would not contend with You, oh God.

Who am I to question Your works? Who am I to say I can do this or that without God's guidance and blessing? Lord, I planted and watered, but You gave the increase.

Thank You, Lord, for a humble spirit. Thank You, Lord, for the wisdom that You have given me, the riches and glory You bestow on me.

Lord, help me never to be boastful in myself, because all that I am or will be, I owe it to Your glory. Lord all that I have received is a gift from You.

I am so thankful, oh God, that I understand that "You are the Lord, the one who exercises loving-kindness and judgment and righteousness in the earth. You are great, and there is none like You," (Jeremiah 10:6) so I will praise You all of my days.

"Do not be proud, for the Lord has spoken. Give glory to the Lord before He causes darkness before You and You stumble" (Jeremiah 13:15). Humble yourself before the Lord.

You have called me by name, oh God. Please do not forsake me, and hear me when I pray, consider my thoughts, and humble me.

Bless me with a heart to be humble before You. Lord, remove all foolish pride from within me. Help me never to boast in myself, because it is You who opens doors for me to walk through, who spread good tables before me.

It is You who lights my way in the darkness, it is You who gives me strength to run and not be weary, to walk and not faint.

It is You who heals me when I am sick, comforts me when I am sad, lifts me up when I am down, so I am thankful that I understand that You are my God worthy of praise.

Dear Lord, Your Word reminds me that "when pride comes then come shame. But with the humble is wisdom" (Proverbs 11:2).

Help me, oh God, to be never too prideful to acknowledge my weaknesses before others. I know, oh Lord, that You hate pride, arrogance, the evil way, and the perverse mouth.

I fear you because of these, so let me always be reminded of where I've been. Let me never forget those who assisted me when I was in need.

Let me remember to give someone else a chance, because my God of second chances has done that for me.

Let me never be too quick to pass judgment on others, knowing that I myself had been there.

Teach me to use soft words that will turn away wrath, and to avoid harsh words that will stir up anger.

"Everyone proud in heart is an abomination to You, oh Lord," (Proverbs 16:5) so help me never to boast in myself.

Remove all traces of arrogance from me. Remove every evil thought from within me, remove all perverseness from my mouth, so that my ways may be pleasing to You.

Oh, that men would understand, that a man's heart plans his way, but the Lord directs his steps. Amen.

Lord, I confess to You today that I have been arrogant and prideful. I need a new start. Humble me.

Because of You

God makes it possible for us to do so many wonderful things. He delivers us from many dangers; He provides for us in special ways. We can do nothing with our own strength.

"Happy is he who has the God of Jacob for His help" (Psalm 146:5). Lord, each day I will lift mine eyes up to You because You are my helper and my help comes from You.

Thank You, Lord, for Your guidance, Your protection, and Your love. Thank You for health and strength, for courage and patience, which enable me to carry out the tasks You have set before me.

It is because of You that I can see the good in every bad situation. It is because of You why I stumble yet do not fall.

It is because of You that I am able to see each new day. It is because of my faith in You that I am able to move mountains. It is because of You, I am strengthened each day for any battle I will face.

It is because of You that my enemies are fleeing seven ways. It is because of You why I am daily drinking from the fountain.

It is because of You that I am able to heap coals of fire on the heads of my enemies. It is because of You who enlighten my way that my burdens are easier to bear.

It is because of You that I am able to step out in faith each day. It is because of You that I have a testimony to share with others. It is because of You my strength is renewed like an ox.

I am blessed in my going out and my coming in because of You, and I always have enough because of You. "Happy is he who has the God of Jacob for His help" (Psalm 146:5).

What have I done to deserve Your help each day, oh God? Give me a prayerful and thankful heart.

Giving Back to God

God gives us so much, yet we give back so little to Him. We have so much, but we don't share with others. We forget that a blessing shared is a blessing multiplied. In whatever way God choose to bless you, render unto Him what rightly belongs to Him. When we give to the poorest of them, know that we are giving to God.

Each day, oh Lord, I come to You in prayer asking for one thing or the other. I have received Your blessings, and I know I am not giving back enough to You.

I know that You love a cheerful giver. Please show me how to give back to You, some of what You have so freely given to me.

In the past You have positioned me to help others; You opened doors for me, so that in return I could open a window for someone else.

Yet, when I felt safe I forgot everyone else. I closed that door when my house was full. I did not remember that a blessing shared was a blessing multiplied.

You give me courage when my faith wavers. You give me strength for the journey. When I am feeling lost and alone You comfort me.

Yet, when I see my brother standing on the road, with a heavy load, and when I see my sister fallen by the way, I just walk the other way.

When I need help to stand, You are always by my side, and when I need to be led by Your guiding hand, You are there to gently direct me.

Yet, I never make time to help the fallen, or to provide direction to the lost, or say to someone, there is a better way.

Lord, You have been my rock and my strong tower. No matter what I have done, no matter where I have been, no matter what I have said, You are the driving force behind it all.

So, when I find myself in a position to help, let me do so with a willing hand, and a cheerful countenance.

Lord, I want to continue on the path that You have set before me. I want to always be pleasing to You, so lead me and guide me in all I do.

I just want You to show me just how I could give back to You, some of what You have so freely given to me, and help me to always remember, that a blessing shared is a blessing multiplied.

Today, I will give with a cheerful heart and help with a willing hand.

Guidance and Direction

A Prayer for Guidance and Protection

God will continue to guide and protect us from all evil, and no matter where we have been, He will re-direct us and keep us on the right path. God's eyes roam the whole earth; He knows where we are at all times and He already knows His plans for us. Every day, we need to pray for His guidance and His protection, pretend that we are building a house, and that He is the architect. God has the blueprints for our lives.

Dear Lord, I come before You this morning, with a prayerful and thankful heart. Lord, You have been walking with me daily, leading me in the right paths. Thank You, dear Lord, for Your guidance and protection in this dark and sinful world.

Thank You for preparing the way before me. I know that You have not forgotten me, I am confident that You will create mountains for me in the midst of valleys and make my wilderness a pool of water.

So teach me to be patient. Teach me to wait upon You, knowing that You, oh Lord, are all powerful, that You will water my thirsty soul with refreshing waters, so that I will be able to tell someone else what Your Holy hand has done for me.

Continue to open my eyes so that I may see Your goodness each day. Lord, Your way is not my way, nor Your thoughts my thoughts, and I am trusting You, therefore, to continually direct my thoughts and actions, I am trusting You for everything in my life.

When I see how You delivered me from the depths of despair and repositioned my life, and when I see where You are leading me, I know I serve an awesome God. I am living proof that my God is a God of second chances.

There are things that I have done in the past that only You could have forgiven. You have broken the sinful chains that held me captive, and the snares that enticed and entrapped me for too long, and with Your help, I will never be the same again.

Lord, I am praying each day for You to keep me on the right path. You have washed me, and cleansed me; You have given me a new life and I know that I could count on Your guidance and protection as I travel through this dark and sinful world.

Lord, I know that Your eyes roam the whole earth. I know that You are watching over me, so "I will not be afraid of the terror by day, or of the pestilence of the dark, because I am abiding under the shadow of Your wings, and no weapon formed against me shall prosper" (Psalm 91:5–6).

Lord, guide me today. Direct me in all I do and say

The Lord— My Driver, My GPS

Our God Positioning System is daily directing our way. Would you go on a road trip without a map or a Global Positioning System? Without one or the other you would have to make countless stops to ask directions or worse yet, get lost and be unable to find your way. I am daily depending on God for direction. He is my GPS, my God Positioning System.

Lord, I am so thankful that You are in control of my life. Thank You that I could depend on You, my GPS, my God Positioning System. Thank You for daily directing my steps. Thank You that I can trust You at every turn in my life.

Lord, I have traveled some dark roads, roads that had forks and dead ends, winding roads with no end. Until one day when I was so lost and alone, did not know which way to go, I heard a voice say, "Follow me. I am Your GPS, Your God Positioning System."

Since that day, I have been walking in Your way. It has brought me trials that made me stronger. It has taken me through storms that almost destroyed me, but I continued to follow Your directions.

Now, I am experiencing joy unspeakable. I could go through each day with a song in my heart and a spring in my step, and it's all because of Your guidance. I know that

You are leading me. I know that I am far from perfect, so I am looking to You daily for direction.

Continue to be my GPS, my God Positioning System. Re-direct my paths from danger, deliver me from evil, lead me out from trouble and temptation, and especially from forbidden fruits, and Lord, sustain me as You promised and I will live.

Continue to me lead and guide me in the right paths, being careful of the turns I take, being watchful for the forks in the road, and when I reach a crossroad and don't know where to turn, I will depend on You, my GPS, my God Positioning System.

My roads may be long and winding today, but I know, oh God, that I will reach my destination because You are leading me.

Show Me the Way

Rather than leaning to our own understanding, we must ask God to show us the way. Do not be conceited; when you have strayed, when you have wandered, when you get lost, or when you are rebellious, ask God to show you the way.

Dear Lord, I am in need of courage to accept the things in my life that I cannot change. I am struggling daily to try to change the things I could; but, there are at times when I get so frustrated, that I become angry and rebellious, and then I would forget to give You thanks and praise in the midst of my struggle. Lord, please show me the way.

Lord, give me the faith and patience I need to withstand my daily trials, because there are some days that are overwhelming, and some days that run smoothly, and I want to be able to thank You and praise You in good times and bad. I tend to criticize You more and praise You less. Lord, please show me the way.

I want to be able to lift You up in praise even when the going is tough. Lord, You show me Your mercy even when I am undeserving; You love me even when I am unlovely. You give me strength and hope in times of trouble, so please show me the way.

When I am sorrowful You comfort me. When I am hungry You feed me. When I am in need I call on You, and You supply my every need. You fill my life with good things—family, friends, good health and Your saving grace and for those I am thankful.

In my daily walk with You, I want You to use me to do Your will. Teach me Your ways so that I could walk in Your truth. When I falter, dear Lord, pick me up and set me straight again. I have been a broken vessel; You are the Master Potter, making me whole again and again, and I know that You will show me the way.

I have wandered far from the fold, and Your outstretched arms embraced me. I have been rebellious, and You forgave me. I have uttered idle words in vain, and You gave me a new song to sing. I have been blind, and You led me. So please dear Lord, continue to show me the way.

Let me find favor in Your sight, dear Lord. Order my steps, oh Lord, because I know that if I am walking in Your way, even though I may stumble, I will not fall. Thank You, Lord, for showing me the way.

I humbly confess today oh Lord, that I am lost and can't find my way, please show me the path You have chosen for me.

Service and Reward

Here I Am, Lord; Send Me

We must never be afraid to do the will of God. Daily put on the whole armor of God, so that you will be ready and willing, to do God's will. The Lord will outfit and position us for any task He set before us so we should be not afraid. He will be with us.

Where should I go today? What should I do today? I have put on the whole armor of God, because I am ready and willing to take on whatever You have set before me, so wherever You lead me oh God, I will follow.

Show me what You would have me do. Use me in whatever way You see fit; You have outfitted me and carefully positioned me for any battle that I will face, so here I am, Lord; send me.

I have put on the helmet of salvation that will protect my thoughts today that will drive my actions. This helmet, will allow me to think before I speak, to pause before I act, so here I am, Lord; send me.

I have put on the breastplate of righteousness that will guard my heart, that will allow me to bring comfort to someone else, that will allow me to lend a helping hand, so here I am, Lord; send me.

Today, I am girded with the belt of truth. I will boldly confess You with my mouth, oh God. I will be honest in all my dealings. I will not be a false prophet, so here I am, Lord; send me.

Today, I am armed with the shield of faith. I will walk by faith and not by sight. I will be able to thank God in advance for my needs. I will not be worried about tomorrow, so here I am, Lord; send me.

Today, I will put on the sandals of peace. Wherever I go today, I will be a peacemaker. I want to be reminded daily that where there is not a talebearer, strife ceases, so here I am, Lord; send me.

Today, I want to lift high the sword of the spirit, which is Your Holy Word. Let me carry it like a lantern before me; so that its beams would illuminate the whole world, so here I am, Lord; send me.

The Lord has carefully outfitted me for the task He has set before me. Where He leads me today, I will follow.

My Year of Jubilee

Do good works so that you may reap the rewards of true worship—your jubilee. "Whatever work your hands find to do, do it with a willing mind" (Ecclesiastes 9:10). Do not work for selfish gain. God loves a cheerful giver. God blesses able hands. I am working daily to reap the rewards of true worship.

Dear Lord, help me to reap the rewards of true worship. I want to be able to see and enjoy my year of Jubilee. Show me the right, and lead me far away from the wrong. Lord, I know that I am drinking favorably from Your cup, and I want to thank You in advance for its overflow.

I want to continue drinking for daily refreshment. I know that You have given me a heart to praise You. I am thankful for the new song in my heart and for blessing me with inner peace.

Lord, I don't always do what is right, even when I know I should. I know that I am not perfect in Your eyes, but I am thankful for Your love, mercy and forgiveness toward me, and I know that You will bless me with provisions and redemption in my year of Jubilee.

Lord, I know that I could only reap my year of Jubilee if I follow Your commandments, and Your good examples. So I am asking You to renew a right spirit within me, so that I could do the things that I should do, in order to reap my year of Jubilee.

Lord, I am so beautifully and wonderfully made. You are always with me. Give me a right spirit to follow Your ways, and Your commandments, so that I may reap the rewards of true worship, my year of Jubilee.

To serve You, oh God, requires me to be obedient to Your word, help me to reap the rewards of true worship.

The Lord Is My Dwelling Place

If God is our dwelling place, let us work to spend eternity in His dwelling place—Heaven. While we are on earth let us do good works that would secure a home for us in God's dwelling place—Heaven.

Lord, You have been my dwelling place I put my trust in You. I will love You from a clean heart and with a pure conscience. Teach me to do Your will, oh God.

Lord, You have been my dwelling place. Give me a forgiving spirit. Help me to forget the past and forgive those who have done me wrong.

Lord, I want to live in peace with You, so teach me to be at peace with myself and to live peaceably with all men. I want to receive Your blessings, so help me to be a blessing to others.

Lord, You have been my dwelling place, so teach me to be a light to shine in the darkness. To help bring those who are living in darkness close to You.

Lord, I am a child of light show me how to walk in the light. Let the fruit of the spirit dwell in me always, so that I may do what is acceptable to You.

Lord, You have been my dwelling place. I will serve You by serving others. I will be loving and kind to all I meet, and I will give You my very best, by giving freely to the poor.

Lord, because You have been my dwelling place, I want to spend eternity with You. So help me to understand Your will. Show me how to live a life that will attract others to You.

Use me as a vessel to spread the Gospel, so that those who do not know You as Lord, Master and Savior, may come to know You in an intimate way.

Lord, You have been my dwelling place. I meditate on Your Word day and night. I strive to keep Your commandments by walking in Your truth.

Lord, I am living by faith day by day. I spend quiet times with You in prayer. You sustain me daily. I know how to wait on You, and because You have been my dwelling place I know I will spend eternity with You in Heaven.

A songwriter Jim Reeves said so true, "This world is not my home, I am just passing through, my treasures are laid up somewhere beyond the blue, the angels beckon me from Heaven's open door and I can't feel at home in this world anymore."

A Prayer for Clean Heart

Let us serve the Lord from a clean heart in order that we may receive His blessings. God knows our hearts, He knows we are frail, He knows that we are tempted in our service to Him. So let us daily ask Him to create in us clean hearts and to renew right spirits within us to serve Him.

Oh Lord, You see what's in my heart. There is nothing hidden from You, so help me to live the kind of life that is honest, loving and true. Create in me a clean heart to praise You, Oh God, and renew a right spirit within me.

Lord Your word reminds me, "He that hath clean hands, and a pure heart; who hath not lifted up his soul unto vanity, nor sworn deceitfully, shall receive the blessing from the Lord, and righteousness from the God of his salvation" (Psalm 24:4–5).

I want to serve You with a pure conscience. I want to be a doer of Your Word and not just a hearer of Your Word. Help me to love my neighbor as myself. Thank You for giving me the discernment, to know right from wrong so that I could be obedient to You.

"Teach me Your ways, oh Lord" (Psalm 86:11) so that I may stand in Your Holy place. Help me to "put on tenderness, kindness, meekness, humility, and long suffering" (Colossions 3:12). Today, Lord, clothe me with compassion, gentleness, and patience.

Erase all traces of jealousy, envy, and malice from me. Remove all thoughts of hatred from me. Let me never put a stumbling block before my brother. Help me to show love to those who differ from me.

You alone can order our unruly minds. You alone have the power to cleanse and make pure, and I know that You have heard my prayer and will create in me a pure heart and give me clean hands so that I will receive Your blessing.

I am depending on You today, oh Lord, to create in me a clean heart.

Expressing Love for God

There are so many different ways for us to express our love for God. Many of us claim that we love God, yet we don't love each other. How could we love God and hate our brothers and sisters? Let us show love for God, by loving one another and by doing loving deeds for each other. I create new ways to express my love for God each day.

"I will continue earnestly in prayer. I will be vigilant in prayer with thanksgiving" (Colossians 4:2). I will continue to serve You oh God by serving others, for in so doing, I will be expressing my love for You.

Lord, I am so thankful for the love that You have given me, a love for self, a love for others, but most importantly, love for You.

I know that I am expressing love for You, oh God, because the things I used to do, I do them no more, the places I used to go, I go there no more, and I am daily telling others all that You have done for me.

I try be patient with others who are different from me and never to turn away from lending a hand to those in need.

Lord, You lift me up when I am down, and in turn I lift someone up who is down. When I am wrong, You humble me so that I could admit my faults.

I am a friend of the friendless, a comfort to those who mourn, the desolate, the oppressed, the orphans and the widows, so that my light will arise in the darkness.

Lord, I lift You up in praise day after day. When I think of Your goodness, oh Lord, when I think of where You brought me from, when I look back at the opportunities You presented to me, I just want to express my love for You.

You protected me. You put a new song in my heart. You watched over my children. Lord, how can I forget to begin and end each day with thanks and praise? How can I forget to express my love for You?

So continue to show me how to serve You by serving others. Lord, teach me to love my neighbor as myself, because in so doing I know that I am expressing love for You.

Position me to serve today, oh God.

Temptation

Prayer for Sexual Temptations

God knows our weaknesses, and He is able to deliver us from all temptations. I will treat my body as a temple of the Lord. I will look to God for the strength to overcome any and all sexual temptations. I will trust Him to show me a way out so as not to give in.

Lord, You know that we have no power within ourselves to help ourselves, and I am asking You to help me to be strong in the face of sexual temptations.

Help me not to follow the desires of my own heart. Help me to hunger only for things that will last like Your love and mercy.

Lord, keep me safe from compromising situations, and help me to treat my body like Your holy temple. Lord, when sexual temptations arise, cover me with Your blood and strengthen me with Your love.

Lord, You know my mind is willing, but my flesh is weak, so cleanse my thoughts, oh God. Help me to focus on things that are lovely, pure, and true. Lead me far away from sexual temptations.

God, I know that You are faithful, and You will not let me suffer sexual temptations above all that I am able to bear; and I believe that with the temptations You will also make a way for me to escape.

Help me to discern the 'wolves' and be my shepherd when they attack. Lord, You know my weaknesses, and I am trusting You to strengthen me, so that I don't give in to sexual temptations and fall into sin. In Jesus' name I pray. Amen.

Help me, oh God, to be tempted and not fall into sin.

Be Angry and Not Sin

Understanding the situations that cause you to get angry, could help you to control your anger, rather than allowing your anger to control you, and cause you to fall into sin. I now fully understand the situations that are most likely to get me frustrated, which cause me to get angry and sin. When I am too hungry, I can't focus. When I am too angry I don't think clearly. When I am too lonely temptations are stronger. When I am too tired I am weak. I am daily seeking God's help to deal with these situations.

Lord, when I get angry, please help me not to sin. When I am tempted to whine or complain, intervene and clear my mind, so that I could refocus my thoughts on pleasant things.

When I am tempted to get angry and sin, because of lack or challenge, help me to walk away from these situations until calm returns.

"For out of our mouths come blessing and cursing" (James 3:10), and this should not be, so give me the right words to say. Help me to bless You and not curse. Help me to ask for Your Grace.

Lord, I know that I need to work on my patience. Because of my lack of patience with situations that challenge me, or people who are different from me, I am tempted to sin in my anger.

Help me to be more understanding with people who are different from me. Send me Your calming spirit in the midst of these challenging situations, so that even if I am tempted to get angry that I would not sin.

"With our tongues we praise You, oh Lord, and with the same tongue we curse men who were made in Your likeness" (James 3:9). I want Christ-like words to come out of my mouth. I want my thoughts and actions to be Christ-like. If I ever sin in my anger, please forgive me.

Lord, I now understand the situations that challenge me. I understand that it's when I am faced with these challenges that I am most likely to fall into sin. So teach me, Lord, how to handle my situations.

Help me never to be too hungry, too angry, too lonely, or too tired. Lord, when I am hungry I can't focus. When I am angry I don't think clearly. When I am lonely temptations are stronger. When I am tired I am weak.

So I am depending on You, oh God, to show me how to deal with these situations, so that when I am challenged, I would remain calm and not sin, to stay focused, to think clearly, and to withstand. Show me how to turn my negative emotions into positives.

Lord, I recognize the emotions that cause me to get angry. I need Your help to control my emotions before they lead me to destruction.

Employment

Prayer in the Face of Layoffs

I now know that God will never close one door unless He has another prepared. I have been laid off from jobs so many times, that I don't worry any more. Not because I have gotten used to it, but every time I get laid off, I always find something more fulfilling. I try to give my best to the job I undertake so that when it ends, I can say with pride, "My work here is done," and thank God for the next job that He has prepared for me.

Dear Lord, I am facing a layoff from my job. I am fearful, oh Lord, even though I know deep within me that I should feast on Your Word, understanding that all things work together for good to those who love You.

But I am only human, oh Lord, I have a family to take care of, I have obligations oh Lord that I am worried about. I know that if I am praying, I should not be worrying, so today I will put my trust in You, because You are my hope and my confidence.

You are my God who promised to supply all of my needs according to Your riches in glory in Christ Jesus. You are my protector, so I will remain in Your presence and wait patiently for You to act.

Lord, I am thanking You for this job, and if my work here is done, I know that You never close one door unless You have another open, and if another door does not open in my timing, help me to understand that You are working Your purpose out.

Give me the wisdom, the patience, and the understanding to wait for Your blessing. Help me to be an encouragement to others even though I am discouraged, and show me how to thank You in the midst of all this.

Help me to keep trusting You for everything. Lord, I can do nothing without You, I am nothing without You, but I know for sure that I can do all things through You, because You strengthen me.

You will lead and guide me through this, so that I will be able to tell someone else, the God I serve is a miracle-working God, who opened doors for me that man can't shut. Thank You, Lord.

Lord, I am believing today that You will never close a door unless You have another prepared for me.

Prayer for a Saved Job

Learn to be content. God promised to meet all of your needs according to His riches in glory in Christ Jesus. God is the doorkeeper of our lives; He knows when to open and close doors for us. He does not need to be tipped; all He requires are grateful hearts. I am grateful, oh God, for doors that You have opened and closed for me. If only we could understand that some doors need to stay closed.

Thank You, dear Lord, for keeping this window of opportunity open for me. I was so worried about being laid off, but I trusted You, and now I am so thankful for this job, so that I will be able to continue to take care of my family.

Lord, how can I thank You? How can I show You how grateful I am for Your marvelous works? Lord, the salary is not much, but it's better than nothing.

You have assured me in Your Word, that if I can manage with little, You will put me in charge of plenty, You remind me to be content in whatever state I am in.

I am asking You to help me to still lend a hand to those less fortunate, to share the little that I have, because all that I have is a gift from You.

You give me more than I deserve, I am counting my blessings daily. I am doing my best to use Your resources rightly.

You want me to be responsible, dear Lord. You want me to be appreciative of every opportunity You send my way.

Help me to be humble to those in authority. Help me to give 100 percent to my job each day.

Help me to be punctual, help me to get up each day thankful for this job and eager to go to work.

I know if I am able to perform in this way, as the Scripture says, "I am working for the Lord, not for men. My reward will come from Him" (Colossians 3:23–24).

Heavenly Father, I am depending on You to show me which door to walk through today or which door to close that I have kept open.

Waiting and Trusting in God for a New Job

When you trust in the Lord you will always have enough. When you find yourself out of a job, and you are waiting and trusting God for something new, use this time for reflection, and a season to cast all of your cares on the Lord. I have done so, and God rewarded me bountifully.

Dear Lord, I have been out of a job for what seems like a long time, and only You know why. It has been a season for me to cast all my cares on You, trusting You to provide for me.

But, Lord, there have been times when my faith wavered, and I became fearful and rebellious. I did not trust You enough to bring me out of my troubles. I did not trust You with my whole heart. I doubted Your love for me.

I forgot that You were the one who carried me many times when I couldn't walk, who fed me when I was hungry, who healed me when I was sick, who brought me out of storms that should have destroyed me.

But, thank You Lord, for keeping me strong in the faith, for refusing to let go of me, for not giving up on me many times when I had given up on myself, Lord, I have been praying and waiting for a new job. My bills have been piling up, but I am never hungry. My budget is stretched, but I always have enough.

For the many times I became fearful and rebellious, when I did not trust You with my whole heart, please forgive me.

For the many times that I have complained about jobs that You have given me instead of thanking You for them, forgive me.

For people who have made life difficult for me in the workplace, who have tried to stop my progress, please forgive them.

Thank You, Lord, for this season of repentance, this opportunity, where I could come humbly before You and ask Your forgiveness for myself and for others.

Lord, when I looked back on all that I have been through, *it was nothing*, compared to the pain and suffering You endured at Calvary for my redemption.

Let me never forget that You were wounded there for my transgressions that You were bruised there for my iniquity.

So, dear Lord, when I am tempted to feel fearful and rebellious, when my faith wavers, let me feel Your nail-scarred hands and feet.

Let me feel the crown of thorns on Your head, and remember the pain You had to bear as You hung and suffered for me at Calvary.

Let me be reminded, that no matter what I am going through at this time, I just need to put my faith and trust in You, and believe You for a stroke of Your blessing.

I know that the same God who created jobs for me in the past could do it again; the same God who sustained me through layoffs will do it again. So position me, equip me dear Lord for the new job that You have prepared for me. In Jesus name I pray. Amen.

Today, I will have favor from the Lord. I will receive a stroke of blessing from the Lord.

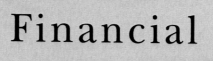

Financial

Prayer for Increase

"To whom much is given, much is required" (Luke 12:48).
When you ask God to bless your increase, seek to find out what
He requires of you. Sometimes we are waiting on God, but
God may be waiting on us. I am so glad that He was patient
enough to wait on me.

Lord, I come before You this morning with a request for
an increase in my finances. I am trying so hard to make
ends meet, but I am just not making enough to meet my
demands. Lord, please show me the way.

Lord, You said Your grace is sufficient. Lord, You
remind me that You will supply all of my needs according
to Your riches in glory, and I am in need of a better paying
job, a satisfying job.

Lord, I am tired of not being able to or barely making
ends meet. I am tired of this struggle day after day. Lord, I
know that You would not give me more than I could bear,
so lift me up and out of this financial situation.

Show me a way to increase my finances. Help me to
live the abundant life, not just financially, I want to be
happy and fulfilled in every area of my life. Lord, I know
that You have been blessing me in special ways, and I keep
asking for more blessings.

I also know that to whom much is given, much is
required, so show me what You require of me, use me as
You see fit, dear Lord, speak to my heart, so that I could

understand and do Your will and be ready to receive Your blessings. In Jesus name I pray. Amen.

I am waiting on You today, oh Lord, for a new job. How would I know if You are waiting on me? Show me what You require of me.

Prayer for Financial Relief

God has given us talents and resources that He wants us to use rightly and to His honor and glory. If you are not using the talents and resources that you were blessed with in the right way, this may be a hindrance to the answer to your prayers. I should know. Ask God to show you how to use your talents and resources rightly to get the results you need.

Dear Lord, I come into Your presence this morning with all of my financial cares. I am putting my mortgage in Your hands, my medical bills, my insurance bills, my credit card bills, my utility bills, and my grocery bills, asking You for a financial relief.

Provide a way out for me, oh God, to meet and exceed my obligations. Help me not to give in to evil and temptation and despair. Lord, I am trusting You for a positive answer, I am seeking Your guidance in this situation.

Lord, I know that I have made financial decisions in the past that were not responsible; forgive me, Lord. I know that You have given us talents and resources and You want us to use them rightly and to Your honor and glory.

If I have been irresponsible in the past, oh God, show me the way I should go; order my steps, and help me to be able to listen to Your still small voice in order to make the right choices, so that I could be financially viable again.

I am confident, that my God of second chances has heard my prayer and will provide for me a financial relief. I am confident, that the same God who blessed me with talents and resources, will show me how to use them rightly. This is my prayer for Christ's sake Amen.

Don't be afraid to ask God to reveal to you your talents and resources so that you could use them rightly.

A Month-End Prayer

God always provides a better way. I have struggled to meet financial deadlines month after month, but I am now convinced that prayer changes everything. When I worry and don't pray, my struggle is great, but when I pray and believe that God will make a way, He makes roadways for me in the wilderness and rivers in the desert.

Thank You, Lord, for closing out another month for me financially. I could not have done it without You. When the month started, I knew it was going to be rough, but I believed that You would see me through. I trusted You; I prayed to You; I thanked You in advance, and You rewarded me.

Lord, help me to continue to meet my financial obligations. Help me to be financially responsible. Lord, You know my financial needs at this time, and I know that You will provide all that I need, so I am thanking You in advance for any and all blessings that You will send my way.

I know that You are going to provide opportunities to increase my finances. I know that You are going to open healthy doors for me to walk through, so, dear Lord, I am thanking You for my job. Please continue to bless me with this stability.

Bless all those who stretch forth their hands to assist me in my times of need. Bless me financially so that I could in turn help someone else. Lord, You provide for me daily in special ways. You bless me with inner peace during my financial storms, and for this I am eternally grateful.

Lord, I know that You want me to be all that You created me to be. I know that I am Yours because You have called me by my name. I know that You have great things in store for me and I believe in my heart, that eyes have not seen or ears heard, nor has it entered into the heart of man what You have in store for me.

So help me to awake each day and look to You, eagerly, expectantly, and thankfully, knowing that You are able to carry me through not only each second, minute or hour of each day, but each day, each month and each year. Thank You, Lord.

Lord, help me to begin the month looking to You eagerly, going through it expectantly and ending it thankfully.

Deliverance

Walking in Darkness

We, who have experienced God's marvelous light, need not walk in darkness anymore. I was walking in so much darkness before I invited God into my heart. I was not only listening to the wrong voices, I was following their directions. Now, the only voice I hear is one that says, "I love you, you are a child of light, walk in the light."

Heavenly Father, I have walked in darkness for a very long time, but thank You for Your son, Jesus, the light of the world.

Because of Him, oh Lord, I am able to see Your marvelous light. This light is like a beacon to my heart.

When I was walking in darkness, I did not know how to pray. When I was walking in darkness, my feet got stuck every step of the way.

When I was walking in darkness, trouble assailed me from every side. My faith was tested at every turn.

When I was walking in darkness, my feet would continually slip and slide. But thank You, for Your son Jesus, for this light, this anchor, this protector.

Heavenly Father, I am so thankful for Your son, Jesus, the light of the world, who showed me the way out of darkness and into His marvelous light.

When I was walking in darkness, I was making bad decisions, when I was walking in darkness I was easily influenced by others.

When I was walking in darkness I was a follower and never a leader. I was listening to the wrong voices, saying things I should not say and doing things I should not do.

But thank You for Your son Jesus, this guide, this everlasting beacon, this light of the world. Because of this light, oh Lord, I stumble, yet never fall.

This light is like a lantern on a dark hill, when my way gets dark and I lose my way, this light shines brighter to show me the way.

This light guides my soul to refreshing waters, this light has moved me from walking blindly, to living by faith and not by sight. Thank You for Your son, Jesus, the light of the world.

No more am I walking in darkness, because of my faith in God, I have seen this great light, and my faith is the fuel for this light.

As my faith grows stronger, this light shines brighter. I know now, that if I am walking in darkness, that God can reveal His glorious light in my darkest hour.

He will provide a light that will be a light unto my feet and a lamp unto my path. Thank You heavenly Father, that I was walking in darkness, but now I am enjoying Your marvelous light.

I will share my lamp with someone else today, that they too could enjoy God's marvelous light.

How Did I Get to This Place?

You have strayed and can't understand how you got to that place. I have found myself in this situation at one point in my life. I can't explain how I got to that place, but a television minister helped me. I had stopped my daily meditation and singing songs of praise to God; I just stopped believing and trusting in God. I happened to turn on the television one Saturday evening and this minister spoke directly to me. He said, "There is someone going through a rough time right now, you used to pray and sing and shout praises to God, but you don't do it anymore." That someone was me; I was tormented all night until I fell asleep. I woke up at 3:00 am, wrote this prayer and went back to sleep. When I woke up again, the answer came to me in the words of the prayer immediately following this one, it also came to me in song.

For many years I have walked in the Christian way, but for some reason, my faith kept slipping each day, and I keep asking myself...

How did I get to this place? Why did I come to this place? Who led me here to this place?

I don't know how; I don't know why. I don't know what I need to do, so wash me in the blood of the lamb.

Oh, cleanse me, refresh me. Wash me whiter than snow. Lead my feet where I should go.

I need to re-focus. I need to plan. I need to hold on to God's unchanging hand.

I felt myself slipping away, further and further each day. I used to sing. I used to sway. I used to pray on my knees all day. But something got a hold of me, something that just wouldn't set me free. But thank God for the cleansing blood that could wash me whiter than snow.

Oh, the blood that Jesus shed for me, this blood that I know could deliver me, Lord take control, and make me whole, lead me out of this place.

Through it all, through it all, I knew who was watching over me. I heard His voice; I felt His touch, but sin's dreaded pull was just too much.

But God is good, and God is great. His healing hand is never late. He led me through that open gate, and I know I'll never turn back, for God has been so good to me. My God delivered me from that place.

When you find yourself in a dark place, instead of giving up, hold on to God in prayer.

I'll Never Go Back
to That Place

When Jesus brings you out of that awful place, you have much to thank Him for. I wrote this prayer, and I sang it over and over again until I felt renewed. I felt so good, I then called my mother and told her what happened and sang the song to her, and we rejoiced together. I have so much to thank God for, I will never go back to that place.

Thank You, Jesus; thank You, Jesus; thank You Jesus I am out of that place. Hallelujah, hallelujah, hallelujah. I'll never go back to that place.

I don't know, I don't know, I don't know, what led me there to that place, but Jesus washed me; Jesus cleansed me; He made me white as snow again.

Thank You, Jesus; thank You, Jesus; thank You, Jesus I am whole once again. Oh, hallelujah, hallelujah, hallelujah. My soul has been reclaimed.

Never more, never more, never more to return to that place; Jesus led me; Jesus guided me; Jesus saved me from that awful place.

Oh, I love Jesus; oh, I love Jesus. Oh, I thank Jesus for restoring me again. I can now sing; I can now shout because Jesus my soul has regained.

Thank You Jesus, thank You Jesus, thank You Jesus, Hallelujah, hallelujah, hallelujah,

I'll never go back to that place, because I have been washed in the blood of the lamb.

Our God is a God of second chances.

Health and Healing

A Healing Prayer

God can bring healing, deliverance, and restoration to all to those who are in need and are humble enough to seek Him out. Learn to pray, not only for yourself, but also for others. I am supported by Prayer Warriors who understand that where two or three are gathered, that God is in the midst. I make it a habit to pray especially for people on my prayer list that God will bring healing, deliverance and restoration to them.

Dear Lord, I come before You this day, asking for Your help in bringing healing, deliverance, and restoration, especially to these people on my prayer list and for those I remember at this time.

Lord, I come to You not in my own might, but in Your strength, and because You are a merciful God, I know that You will incline Your ear to my prayers as I lift them up to You, and trust You completely to make every path smooth, every crooked way straight, and for everyone who is bowed down, to be lifted up.

Lord, You are the Great Physician, our source of comfort and all good things. Give us thankful hearts each day, so that despite our struggles we could lift You up in prayer. Lord, it is so easy for us to become fearful in the face of adversity; it is so easy for us to turn away from You, trusting You when our backs are against the wall.

We forget You, oh God, in times when we should be remembering You, calling on You, drawing down on Your strength, but we are human, oh God and humans forget, so remind us; remind us to cast all our cares on You, to lay our burdens at Your feet, to give them over to You, those things that we have tried to fix ourselves and have failed, forgetting that You are our burden bearer.

Lord, this day, I bring before You all those who are sick in mind, body, and spirit, those who are in trouble, those who are homeless, those who are without jobs to sustain their families, those who are struggling with addictions.

Lord, lift up those who are discouraged and lost; help them to find their way; help them to see and to know that in You is fullness of joy, that in You is sweet peace, and that trusting and believing in You has great rewards.

Today, as we bring our burdens laying them at Your feet, we are believing and thanking You for healing, deliverance, and restoration. We are believing that Your hand is not too short to save us, nor Your ears too heavy to hear our cries. All this we ask in the powerful name of Jesus. Amen.

I am thanking You today, oh God, for healing, deliverance and restoration for all those who are in need at this time.

Prayer for Medical Test Results

God is our Great Physician. I am not fearful when I pray, because I know my Great Physician is always near, with a sympathizing and understanding ear.

Lord, do not desert me now. You alone are my hope. Look down favorably on me, and let my test results be good, or reveal something that could be corrected or controlled. I know, oh Lord, that You are the Great Physician.

You alone can help and heal. You alone see and understand all things, and that is why I could boldly say, "speak Lord and Your servant shall be healed," Lord bless me with enough faith to make me whole.

Remove every doubt and fear from within me, oh God. Fix my thoughts on You. Lord, this day I will choose whom I will serve, and I know that I serve a God who hears and answers prayers, a miracle-working God.

I know that I could count on You in every situation in my life. I know, dear Lord, that You are my strong deliverer, my Great Physician. Lord, You ordered Naaman to wash in the Jordan seven times. Tell me what I need to do seventy times, and I will.

I am trying to be obedient to Your every Word. I am waiting patiently for You to raise my Lazarus. I am waiting patiently to be touched by You. I am waiting patiently for You to heal me from the inside out.

Lord, by Your stripes we are healed. Lord, by faith we could move mountains, and I know that if it is Thy will, I will be made whole again. So thank You, Lord; thank You, Lord; thank You, Lord.

Lord, I don't know what I am facing today, so speak Lord and your servant shall be healed.

Prayer for Mother

God will preserve the faithful.

Heavenly Father, I come to You this day, prayerful for my mother. Lift her up from her sick bed. Make her well, dear Lord. Keep her safe through this storm of life. Lord, You see and know all things. Give her the peace that surpasses all understanding.

Let her find rest in You, oh God. Lord, give her the chance to complete her work here on earth. Take away the demon of fear from her, the demon of worry and the demon of anxiety. Lord, when we are weak, we can count on Your strength.

Lord, there is no love like a mother's love. There is no understanding for a child like a mother. Thank You, Lord, for the blessings of my mother. Thank You that I was blessed with a God-fearing mother, a mother who taught me about God from my youth onward, a mother who instilled good values in me, a mother whose words of wisdom I pass on to my children.

Lord, You love those who do Your will. Mother has been doing Your will. Mother has been faithful to You, and I know that You have the power to preserve her, oh God. Let this cup pass from her. Lord, we are grown, but we still need her. She is our sounding board for our dreams, our support in times of trouble, and our dose of reality when needed.

Lord, not my will, but Thy will be done. Whatever it is that you need her to see during this illness, reveal it to her. Help her to commune with You from her sick bed. Let her be in the right frame of mind to receive Your understanding, in Jesus' holy name I pray. Amen.

If we are faithful to You, oh God, You will not allow our strength to fail in times of adversity.

Prayer for a Sister

You could be an inspiration to someone else going through trials. If you could empathize with someone going through a trying time in their life, you could help to make their journey easier to bear. Help them to focus on the positive things in their lives rather than the problem, and give God thanks.

Thank You, dear Lord, for the blessings of a sister. Lord, I bring my sister before You, as You know her heart. You see what she is going through, but I know, dear Lord, that all things work together for good to those who love You. Lord, I am lifting her up to You and asking You to increase her faith.

Help her to understand that You will never give her more than she could bear. Give her the wisdom to understand her situation, and to accept what she is going through by thanking You despite the problem; by thanking You for the support and encouragement of a loving family, by thanking You for the good things in her life.

Lord, I have experienced tribulations, and I have learned to trust You and thank You in the midst of it all, and You have delivered me from many storms. So help me to be a blessing to my sister, to help her understand that You are not finished with her yet, that her life is work in progress.

Give her strength for the journey, bless her with inner peace. Fix her thoughts on You and not her problems. Remind her that Your grace is sufficient. Lord, Your ways are not our ways, but we know that You are an on-time God, that You hear and answer every prayer.

Help her not to complain but to wait patiently for Your answers, and if the answers are delayed keep her earnest in prayer, believing that You, oh God, can do more than we could ever ask or deserve, and that You will always give us our fruits in due season. Thank You, Lord for the blessings of a sister.

Dear God, I will fix my thoughts on You today and not my problems.

Prayer for the Sick

"They that wait upon the Lord shall renew their strength"
(Isaiah 40:31). When we are sick and ask for God's healing, it's
how we wait, that determines how our strength is renewed.
We must never get weary, anxious, or tired.

Dear God, we come humbly before You this day, not only because we have a need, but in thanksgiving for the wonderful signs and miracles that You reveal to us each day, and we are thanking You today for complete healing for the sick and suffering.

We are opening the door of communication to You, oh God, and not only to voice our prayers and supplications, but to listen to Your still, small voice. Help us to hear the voice of You our Shepherd and to stand ready to Your call.

We come to You in prayer, oh God, confident that You will answer our prayers to heal the sick and suffering. Help us not to get weary or tired or agitated as we await the answers to our prayers. Lord, help us also to recognize that You are an on-time God.

If we are praying and it seems like nothing is happening, enlighten our way so that we could understand, that if You delay in answering our prayers that it is for our own good. Help us to be in tune with Your timetable, understanding that You know exactly what we need and most importantly, when we need it.

Help us to learn to be prayerful in the midst of our trials; show us how to really give You thanks and praise when our burdens are heaviest, because in these times, oh God, we are weak, and Your Word reminds us that even when we are weak that we are strong, because You are with us and You promise to never leave us nor forsake us.

Dear Lord, when we are facing the trials and tribulations of this life it is so easy to turn away from You, but in this situation, dear God, we realize how much we need You, that You are the Great Physician and that only You can do the impossible.

So, dear God, as we lift up the sick and suffering before You, we are confident that our prayers have not gone unheard, and that is why we could boldly say thank You, dear Lord, for this situation that is bringing us to You in prayer. You have our undivided attention, so we will be still in Your presence and wait patiently for You to act.

"Oh, they that wait upon the Lord shall renew their strength; they shall mount up with wings like eagles; they shall run and not be weary; they shall walk and not faint" (Isaiah 40:31), so teach us, Lord, to wait on You and to trust You completely for the healing of the sick and suffering, in Jesus' holy name I pray. Amen.

Lord, we will thank You today in advance for the answer to our prayer.

Prayer through Pain

The Lord will turn our pain into praise, so we should hold on in prayer. His Word reminds us in Psalm 30:5 that weeping may endure for a night or two, but that joy will come in the morning.

Help us to understand Oh Lord, that there is a reason for our pain, that there is pleasure in our pain, that there is healing for our pain, and that there is deliverance in our pain.

We know, oh Lord, that You will never give us more than we can bear. You know when we are in pain, You understand the reasons for our pain, You care about our pain, and You will restore us again.

Help us, dear Lord, to always understand that there is a reason for our pain. Our pains make us stronger. Our pains bring us closer to You; they increase our faith in You; they give us a testimony to share.

When we are in pain, we cry out to You, oh God. Help us to hold on in prayer. Help us to understand that nothing lasts forever, that this pain too shall pass, just like a woman in labor, who forgets her misery, when her child is born.

Show us how to understand our pains. Reveal to us the reason for our pains. Help us to be courageous and strong in our pains, believing that You will bring us deliverance from our pains.

Lord, if our faith is small and our strength fails in the day of adversity, help us to "rejoice in our sufferings and to endure our tribulations, knowing that these will produce perseverance, character and hope that will never disappoint us" (Romans 5:3–5).

Lord, my pain and suffering is nothing compared to what You endured for me at Calvary.

Family

A Prayer for Fathers

We know that You oh God can bring positive change to any situation. I am a single parent, and I have seen disappointment in my child's eyes more times that I would like to remember. I tried to shield her from her father so she won't have to deal with this hurt, but it never goes away. For years I tried to handle this in my own strength; it did not work. But as I have grown in my walk with God, I have come to forgive her father and pray for him, and by asking God to heal the relationship. My daughter is grown, but still longs for a relationship with her father. I just want to say a special thank you to my family for the support and love that my daughter and I receive each day.

Dear God, I am thankful that I have a father in You, a father who corrects me, directs me, and instructs me. There are many children today lacking the support of a father, and they are going astray because they have no one to bring them up in the right way.

Dear God, children need love, support, and guidance from their parents. For those fathers who neglect their children, who have abandoned them, who offer no support or encouragement, who fail to instruct their children as the Lord commands, I am lifting them up to You, oh God, because only You can bring change to any situation. Only You can order our unruly minds.

Children need the support and encouragement of a father. No parent should be left to raise a child on their own, and I am praying, oh God, for mothers who are bringing up their children alone, who are struggling to bring them up in the right way, to give them over to You, to direct, to correct, and to instruct them, oh God, because You care for them; You love them.

I am confident that You will be a father to the fatherless, because Your Word reminds us "to never despise Your chastening, nor detest Your correction for whom the Lord loves He corrects" (Proverbs 3:11).

My prayer to You today oh God, is for You to turn the hearts of every father, who for whatever reason is not there for his children, to reopen the door of communication between them, and move their hearts to do the right for their children.

Children do not choose their parents, and parents do not choose their children; God, You did, and if anyone could heal, restore, and renew these relationships, it's You, oh God, so this is my prayer in Jesus' name. Amen.

Children need the support and encouragement of their fathers. Help me, oh God, to pray each day for healing, restoration, and renewal of these relationships.

A Prayer for Our Children

Our children are in need of our prayers for guidance and protection every day. When you pray for them, remember to call them by their names.

"Children are an heritage of the Lord" (Psalm 127:3), and as I bring my children before You this morning, I give You thanks and praise, and I lift them up to You, oh God, asking You to use them as a channel of Your love.

Bless them in their going out and their coming in. Help them to recognize, oh God, that their lives are not their own and that You will prepare the best pathway for their lives and allow You to work Your purpose out.

I call them by name, asking for health and healing, prosperity, guidance, and protection. Help them to give their best in their daily life and work, and help them to be honest and fair in all they do and say.

Move in their hearts to be a blessing to others, even as You have blessed them. Help them to understand that all things come from You, oh Lord, and that all that they have or will be they owe it to Your glory.

Lord, whatever the direction they take in life, take a step before them and lead them in the right paths. They may falter and stumble along the way, but I know that Your right hand will hold them up.

I know that Your outstretched arms are around them. Cover them with Your blood, oh God, as they go out each day in this dark world of sin so that they can discern right from wrong.

Dear God, children need role models. Provide good people in their lives. People who could provide inspiration for them; people who could mold them and help them to grow; people who could instill good values in them; people who could help them to achieve their goals and not people to hold them back.

Lord, every day is a learning experience. Teach them to be respectful to those in authority and to accept constructive criticism gracefully. Broaden their minds to accept new things and increase their knowledge so that they can understand all things.

"The fruit of the womb is your reward" (Psalm 127:3), so wherever my children are at this time, oh God, my hands and feet cannot reach them, but I know that my prayers will, and I ask Your blessings on them for Jesus Christ's sake. Amen.

Lord, please hear my prayer for my children as I individually lift them up to You.

Prayer for a Child's Birthday

Speak positive words over your children so that God can bless them in every area of their lives.

Thank You, Lord, for blessing me with this wonderful child celebrating another birthday today. Bless her in special ways, oh God; watch over her, be her guide and her protector in her going out and coming in and shield and defend her from all assaults of the enemy.

Lord, provide a way for her to finish her education, and help her to see the positive in every negative situation. I know that You will secure jobs for her that will satisfy and fulfill her, that You will provide opportunities that could promote her, and send good people in her life to motivate her.

Dear Lord, children should obey their parents, for it is right. Thank You, dear Lord, for the respect she shows. Children don't always listen, but I am thankful, dear Lord, that she listens, even when she does not agree with me.

For those children that don't listen, for those children that don't show respect for their parents, for those children who are failing in school, for those children who are not successful in their jobs, I remember and lift them up to You, oh Lord.

Give them hearts to praise You. Show them how to see the good in others even when they are hurting. Remind them that they were beautifully and wonderfully made, that they are Your children and that You want the best for them, so lead them in the right paths.

Dear Lord, we ask Your blessings specifically on this child celebrating her birthday today. Give her the strength and courage and patience she needs to continually walk in Your ways, to give her very best to You for Your glory, and bless her to see many more birthdays, for Jesus Christ's sake. Amen.

Today, I will speak positive words over my children so that God will bless them in every area of their lives.

The Husband Prayer

Be specific in your prayer needs, learn to ask, seek, and knock. God knows what we are in need of, and He never gets tired of listening to our requests. When the time is right, He will answer our prayers. I have been praying to God for a husband, and I am still in waiting.

Dear Lord, You promise to answer every prayer when we ask, seek, and knock, and I come to You today earnestly asking You to provide a husband for me.

I believe dear Lord that I don't have a husband, because I did not know how to ask of You. I believe I did not find a husband because I was looking in the wrong places, and knocking on the wrong doors.

Today, I am making my request known to You, oh God, You ask me to be specific in my prayer, so teach me how to ask aright so that You will hear and answer my prayer.

I need a godly man. I need a man who is healthy. I need a man who would be energized to provide for our family. I need a man who would compliment my life and allow me to be me.

That man would love, honor, respect, and cherish me. That man should be caring and devoted enough to anticipate my needs and concerns before I ask.

That man would help build my confidence and not erode my self-esteem, comfort me when I am sad, defend me at all times, support me in my endeavors, and motivate me to be all that I could be.

That man should be honest and true, kind and loving, patient and forgiving, encouraging and stimulating but never controlling or manipulative.

If this is Your will for my life, dear Lord, position me in the right place to meet that man and reveal him to me.

Lord, You've said in Your Word that "it is not good for the man to be alone" (Genesis 2:18), and I know that just as You created Eve for Adam, You have created an Adam for me, and I am trusting You for this blessing in Jesus' holy name. Amen.

Dear Lord, I am trusting You to provide the husband I need if this is Your will.

Prayer for a Troubled Marriage

I believe that the family that prays together stays together. When your marriage is falling apart and love has gone out the window, call on God, and He will be your mediator.

Lord, my prayers go up to You at this time, for all those who are struggling with division in their homes, whose family is in distress because of a troubled marriage, for those struggling with separation, anxiety and divorce, provide peace for them.

Lord, Your Word reminds us that "whom You have joined together to let no one separate" (Mark 10:9). Lord, when we enter into a covenant of holy matrimony, help us to respect the sanctity of this union before You, and be able to stand united at all times.

Lord, I believe that the family that prays together stays together. We forget to put You front and center in our relationships, oh God. We forget to thank You for each other every day. We lose the respect we have for each other because we don't love from a pure heart.

"Love suffers long and is kind; love does not envy, love does not parade itself and is not puffed up, does not behave rudely, does not seek its own. Love is not provoked and thinks no evil, does not rejoice in iniquity but rejoices in the truth" (1 Corinthians 13:4–6).

Lord, teach us to bear each other's burdens, to forgive each other when we fail, even as You have forgiven us. Teach us to be humble and respectful to each other and submitting to one another in the fear of God, for it is right.

"Love bears all things, believes all things, and hopes all things. Love never fails" (1 Corinthians 13:7), so let us be reminded that we are not perfect, that the mind is willing but the flesh is weak, that we must pray to God always to lead us not into temptations, and to deliver us from all evil.

So, dear God, we come to You in prayer, trusting You to restore failing marriages. We are trusting You to bring stability and peace to the families facing separation, divorce and anxiety.

For those whose relationships have run their course, bring them closure, oh God, because two people can only walk together if they are in agreement. This is my prayer in Jesus' name. Amen.

Heavenly Father, I need stability in my home, my family is in distress, grant us peace.

Prayer for Family Gathering

Our families are often spread across many continents, but we will continually pray for and thank God for each other, so that all our needs are met and for unity. We don't often get to celebrate family events together, so we should make the most of these opportunities.

Oh, how good it is when brothers and sisters dwell together in the Lord. Thank You, Father, for the opportunity to be with family again. Continue to unite us in love, use us as vessels for Your glory.

Lord, You know that as family we may have our ups and downs, but I am asking You, dear Lord, to renew right spirits within us, so that we could always be honest to each other, respectful to each other's feelings, be there for each other, and be forgiving one to another.

I am so thankful for this family You have given me, especially my parents, my children, my brothers and sisters and their families. Give them grace so that they may follow Your good examples, provide for them in special ways, and give them thankful hearts, so that they could praise You even in the midst of their struggles.

Thank You, Lord, for the blessings of family. Continually bless the ties that bind us. Help us to continually pray for each other, that we will continue to be blessed by You in special ways. All this I ask for Jesus Christ's sake. Amen.

Dear God, bless my family today, in special ways.

Crisis

Prayer through Crisis

We do not know when a crisis situation will arise, but we know that we are God's children, and that we are abiding under the shadow of His wings.

Dear Lord, thank You for protecting us through this crisis. We know that You are in control of this situation, so we are looking to You for the strength to go on. Lord, to us, this crisis is a burden on all our resources at this time, but we know that You will provide the help that we need to get through this. Where do we begin to make things right again? We are a country in crisis.

Lord we are in need of stability, we are in need of direction, we are in need of guidance on how to move forward, and most importantly we are in need of basic commodities, so please send us the right resources to meet our needs.

We believe in our hearts, that as You provided food and water for the children of Israel when they were most vulnerable; as You shielded them from the enemy; as You parted the Red Sea to allow them to flee safely; and as You guided their every step, day and night, we have every confidence that You will provide for Your children during these difficult times.

You made us, oh God; we are Your children, and Your Word reminds us that "You will never leave us nor forsake us" (Hebrews 13:5), and as a father cares for His children, we know that we are abiding under the shadow of Your wings.

In due time, oh God, You will spread calm over this land. You will restore it to its former glory—lush, vibrant, flourishing, and even more prosperous than before. When the dust settles permanently, we would look back and give You thanks and praise, knowing that if it was not for You on our side, we would not have been here.

So thank You, Lord, for this crisis that has kept us on our knees, that has kept us prayerful, vigilant, and watchful as we should be in preparation for Your second coming. Glory be to God.

Thank You, Lord, for protecting us through this crisis.

Peace Be Still

The Lord will provide peace for us through all our storms of life. I had a situation in my life when I was so worried, so afraid, and I experienced a chastisement from the Lord in three consecutive days. I was humbled. The first day I opened my Bible to begin my meditation, God told me in Matthew 6:25: "Do not worry about your life, what you will eat, drink or wear." The next day I was still afraid, and He told me in Mark 4:39–40: "Peace be still; why are you so fearful; how is it that you have no faith?" The third day I was still fearful. When I began my meditation, the song came to me "Leaning on the Everlasting Arms," and the Psalm that followed was Psalm 121:1: "I will lift up mine eyes unto the hills, from whence cometh my help." What more did I need to hear? Friends, don't let God have to chastise you in this manner, trust Him with all your heart, listen to Him, and He will provide peace for you through all of your storms.

Dear Lord, You are our peace in times of storms. You are our peace in times of disasters. In You we could find peace to overcome our fears, so we will remain faithful during our times of storms. In these our times of trouble, and great tribulation, peace be still.

Lord, we are living in troubled times. We are living in fear, not only of natural disasters, but especially of man-made disasters. Lord, there is so much unrest in the world, so much anxiety in the world. Peace be still.

Lord, we have become an environmentally destructive nation. Major catastrophes are threatening our existence. Day by day we face threats of bio hazards, oil spills, soil erosions and underground mines. They threaten to swallow our streets and produce receding tides, low sea water levels and epidemic outbreaks, but, Lord, we are still here.

So we come before You, oh God, because we know that You would provide peace in all our storms, that You will protect us through all our storms, whether they be hurricanes, volcanic eruptions, tornadoes, hail and wind storms, fires and floods, earthquakes, or famine. We know that we could depend on You for protection.

Thank You, Lord, that we could be safe in our times of storms, that we could be sheltered in our storms, that we could trust You for calm in our times of storms. We know that You rebuked the wind and said to the sea "Peace be still," and the winds ceased and there was great calm.

We will not be afraid. We will continue to trust You to provide peace for us in our storms. We know that You created this beautiful earth, that You created us, that You love us, and that You will protect us in our times of storms. "Peace be still."

When I am anxious, worried or afraid, let me find peace in You, oh God.

Pets

Prayer for Pets

God is our Great Interpreter; He understands all languages, even our pets. I have had pets who were sick and died, and it was heartbreaking to watch them and not being able to help.

Creator of the universe, You created animals to compliment the beauty of the earth, and You created some for our companions.

I have adopted one of Your creatures to be my friend and protector, and although she is but a dumb beast, from her actions, I know she is not feeling well.

We know You understand all languages; You are the great interpreter; so reveal to us what is wrong with her, so that we could treat her and get her well.

Lord, she is only my pet, but she is Your creation, and I know that You want her to be well. So bless her with good health from this day forward. Amen.

What an awesome God we serve.

Travel

Prayer for Travel

Use the opportunity to travel to spread the good news of Christ. No matter where we may go in life, there is always someone who doesn't know Christ, someone who is spiritually hungry.

Lord, You created the heavens and the earth. You separated the sea from dry land.

You divided night from day, and You created man in Your own image and likeness.

And as Your child prepares to travel this great earth, whether by land, sea, or air, I am asking You to spread Your protecting arms around her.

Take her safely to her destination. Let her travels be another opportunity for her to enjoy the beauty of the earth.

Present opportunities for her to tell others of Your goodness. Lord, we know that all over the world, there are people who are spiritually hungry, people who do not know You, people who don't believe.

Lord we are reminded in Your Word that "we should aim to preach the gospel, so that to whom Christ was not announced that they shall see and to those who have not heard so that they will understand" (Romans 15:20–21).

So help her to be an ambassador for You during her travels. Give her courage to spread the good news to those who do not believe, those who have not heard or seen, and then bring her safely back to us. In Jesus' holy name I pray. Amen.

Wherever I go today, oh God, use me as vessel to spread the good news without fear or shame.

Seasonal

A Good Friday Prayer

Good Friday is a promised reminder that Jesus died for us at Calvary so that our sins may be forgiven.

As we gather to celebrate another Good Friday, let us stop to reflect on what this day really means to us. On this day God gave His only son to die on the cross, so that we who believe in Him could have life everlasting.

Good Friday is a promised reminder that our God has made a way for us sinners to come boldly before Him and repent and be forgiven of all our trespasses.

Good Friday is a promised reminder that God did not spare His only Son, so that through His death on the cross and by His rising to life again that we are more than conquerors, that we will never need an excuse to come to Jesus.

Let us be thankful for this day, for Calvary and for Jesus' death on the cross for us. As a result we are free; we are made whole; we have been washed in the blood of the lamb. Because of Calvary, Salvation is ours.

Jesus, You endured shame for us when You went to Calvary, so let us never be ashamed to tell Your story. May we never be ashamed to proclaim the gospel of Christ. May we never be afraid to confess You before men.

When we are burdened and heavy laden, lead us to Calvary, to that special place where we could leave our burdens at Your feet, where we could bare our souls to

You without shame or conviction. Thank You, Jesus, for Calvary and for dying on the cross for us.

I will never be afraid to confess You before men, because of all You endured for me at Calvary.

Celebrating a Season of Joy

Be mindful of the reason for celebrating a season of joy. Let us not forget that Jesus is the reason for the season.

As we celebrate this season of joy, let us remember the reason for the season; because of Jesus' birth, we are renewed, we are marked as joint heirs with Him.

This season should be celebrated fully to His honor and glory. We are so thankful that You came into this world to save us sinners, You love us unconditionally, and You remind us that we also should love one another.

So help us to lend a hand this season to the less fortunate. We know that we are limited in money, we don't have gifts to share, but we could still bring help in some other form to someone else in need.

Help us to remember the poor, the homeless, the destitute, those who are in prison, and in the hospital; for God assures us in Scripture, "that if we offer food to the hungry and satisfies the needs of the afflicted, our light shall rise in the darkness" (Isaiah 58:10), and God's promises are true.

We know that we have been blessed in so many ways, and as You continue to bless us, help us to be a blessing to others, help us to continually thank You for the things that we do have and not worry or complain about the things we don't have.

Lord, there are so many this season that have to do without. There are so many who are too worried about their future and their families, to celebrate this wonderful season of joy. I know that You will make a way for them.

Lord, help us not to worry about tomorrow, about bills to be paid, or not having enough. Just bless us with inner peace, and supply just what we are in need of today, to celebrate this season of joy.

You have given us our Emmanuel, a symbol that You are always with us, so we know that You will position us in the right frame of mind, to focus on the birth of our King, Jesus, the real reason for celebrating this season of joy.

Today, as I celebrate the real reason for this season of joy, I will also remember the less fortunate.

A Christmas Day Prayer of Thanksgiving

Let us be thankful to God for His goodness today. We have so much to be thankful for, so we will begin by thanking Him for His son Jesus our Prince of Peace.

Thank You, dear Lord, for this Christmas Day, for giving us Your Son Jesus, the savior of the world, our Prince of Peace, our hope, and our joy. "His name will be called Wonderful, Counselor, Mighty God, Everlasting Father" (Isaiah 9:6).

Lord, I am lifting You up especially today in praise, because if it was not for Jesus' birth at Bethlehem, if it was not for the manger where He lay, we would not be able to celebrate this glorious day.

So, thank You Lord for the ability to pray, and thank You for the utterance each day. Help me, Lord, to always put You first in all I do, and let me never forget to give You thanks for all the many blessings You bestow on me.

Lord, I know that You are walking daily with me. I know that You are meeting my every need. Lord, when I see how You provide for me each day, and all through the year, I just want to give You all the thanks and praise due Your name.

Lord, I know that You fill my life with good things. You bless me daily, so that I may be a blessing to others.

Use me as a channel to bring others to Christ. Help me each day to share my testimonies with others who don't know You as the Prince of Peace, so that they may glorify You and give You praise.

Lord, I am thankful today for Your guidance and protection, for watching over me, for food on my table, for clothes on my back, for a roof over my head and for family and friends to share with.

I am so thankful oh God, for this day that we celebrate in Your son's name. Let us be joyful and adore Him. Let us never forget to put Christ back into Christmas.

Oh, come let us adore Him Christ the Lord.

Prayer for the New Year

Face the New Year challenges with courage. When we have had a rough year, we are fearful of the unknowns of the New Year. Help us oh God to learn to put You ahead of every challenge that we will face this year, and trust You for favorable outcomes.

This morning, Lord, I am thankful for the dawning of a New Year; a New Year that I know will not only be filled with challenges, but a New Year that will provide opportunities for me to grow spiritually, financially and emotionally.

I could thank You in advance, oh Lord, for the assurance that You will hold my hand and guide me in the right paths. Thank You for the assurance that I will be able to face any and every challenge with courage, knowing that I am not alone, that You will be my stronghold in the day of trouble.

Lord, the past year was trying; I've had many ups and down, but Your goodness and mercy steered me through. I had to make do with little and sometimes had to go without, but I am thankful for my contented state and that I have learned to feast on Your Word.

Lord, I know that I am not perfect. I have stumbled, and I have strayed, but You picked me up each and every time. My faith grew stronger with each challenge I overcame, and I was encouraged by Your love. When I failed, You always showed me another way, a better way, Your way.

Help me to be thankful this New Year for everything. I will be thankful for a job, thankful for my family, thankful for health, thankful for strength, thankful for shared mercies, thankful for disappointments, thankful for troubles, thankful for trials, thankful for joys, thankful for pains, but mostly thankful for the gift of life and Your love. Amen.

God will give you strength and courage for the journey. Just remember to thank Him along the way.

Prayer for New Year Direction

Thank God in advance for direction and the new opportunities He will send our way. He knows what we need, and He has the plan for our lives. Trust Him with all your heart.

Lord I need Your guidance; I am in need of direction for this New Year. Position me for good things, open new doors for me to walk through, and make smooth and straight the road that I will walk.

Lord, this year is new, and I know that You will work Your purpose out for me. Lord, continue to lift me up when I am down, pick me up when I fall. Lord, I know that You understand my weaknesses; help me to be strong in the faith.

Lord, I want to continue walking in Your way, I am depending on You to direct my steps, and I want to continue trusting You with my whole heart. Lord, I can see Your goodness all around me each day, and I know that I can trust You for my every need.

Lord, it has been years of ups and down, troubles and trials, heartaches and pains, but You have been with me. You have seen my successes and my failures. You have seen my comings and goings. I know where You brought me from, dear Lord, I don't know where You will take me this year, but where You lead me I will follow.

I want to begin and end this New Year with You in prayer. I want to thank You for all the many blessings of this life. Thank You for health, family, and home. Thank You for good friends and good neighbors. Thank You for food on my table, and for the strength to go forward this year with an attitude of gratitude, for Christ' sake. Amen.

Lord, please guide my steps and direct my paths this New Year. I want to begin this New Year with an attitude of gratitude.

Prayers for Everyday Living, by Jewellyn
Greer is available wherever books are sold as
both a printed book or an audio book

For more information about the book
including information about speaking
engagements, please e-mail the author

prayersforeverydayliving@hotmail.com

Follow us on facebook for daily
inspirational posts and updates

http://www.facebook.com/PrayersforEverydayLiving